The Man Who Crossed THE TRACKS

The Story of Ray Morland

by Pamela Hatton

Dedications

I would like to dedicate this book to my parents Leo William "Bill" Morland and Margaret Mary "Maggie" Curran, who made many sacrifices to give my brothers (Bill and Kevin), sisters (Margaret and Eileen) and I the best start in life. I dedicate this book also to my best friend and wife, Lynn. Also, to my late stepson, Paul Frederick Blackbee, who contributed to this book, and his sons Sean Landon Blackbee and Jason Hunter Blackbee. I salute the four men of significance: Tom the Barber, PAS, Jim Caughley and Eric Atkinson.

Acknowledgements

Thanks are due to those who have contributed to this book, including those who have contributed testimonials. Appreciation is extended to Brenden D Tempest-Mogg and Julian Ng for their thoughtful suggestions, encouragement and ongoing support to make this book possible. Last, but not least, I would like to thank Dr Pamela Hatton for turning my ramblings into cohesive sentences.

First edition, November 2017.

Warnborough Publishing
18 Lower Bridge Street, Canterbury, Kent CT1 2LG

Additional editing by Julian Ng.

ISBN: 978-0-9568667-5-2

Chapters

Page left intentionally blank

Foreword

How does one begin to tell the story of a man who had a vision of being educated, without fully understanding that vision? A man who had learned from a very young age, the true meaning of helping his fellow man, without recognising that truth until many years later!

There is an educational thread which runs through everything he has attempted to achieve, and has achieved, in his lifetime; and it (his lifetime) is not over yet! Dr Morland's inspirational and motivational attitudes to his fellow human beings are outstanding. He has broken down the barriers between different cultures, establishing solid, educational programmes for indigenous communities, and has dared to stand up to indifference amongst his peers.

In New Zealand, Dr Morland developed special programmes to enhance the poor self-image of the correctional inmates. At the Western Australian Institute of Technology (now Curtin University), he developed the degree course in Social Administration. He also undertook numerous consultancies on a voluntary basis to assist the elderly, the homeless youth, and the Aboriginal Australian, by establishing special educational courses, which are used even now, as the model for the development of the Aboriginal Support Services at most Australian Colleges and Universities.

Not bad for a young boy who first mixed with people from diverse cultures at the tender age of five years, loved the experience then, and embraces it still today!

Dr Pamela Hatton

Appreciation

This book is about a man with a message – a man who overcame many obstacles to acquire an education. This man, Ray Morland, grew up in New Zealand in hard times, yet he faced every hurdle with confidence and determination. His journey in life is an inspiration for those who wish to learn, and acquire an education that will elevate their career and improve their life.

Ray has been associated with Warnborough College since 1999 when we met in Newcastle, Australia. His enthusiasm to become involved with Warnborough was remarkable. When he heard about its history and achievements, he volunteered his services. He expressed a desire to be part of its global vision. Since then, Ray has been active in promoting Warnborough at all levels. With a life-time of experience in higher education, counselling and quality assurance, Ray has been a stalwart and valued Secretary of the Warnborough Council. He has attended its meetings and graduations in Australia, China, Thailand, Philippines, Malaysia and the United Kingdom.

It is an honour and privilege to know Ray, and to appreciate what he has done and achieved for Warnborough, and for the countless students guided to education throughout his life.

"Do not waste your life on folly,
Live to learn, and learn to live.
If you want to pass on knowledge,
You must acquire it first."

Dr Brenden D Tempest-Mogg
President
Warnborough Worldwide

Chapter One
1925 – 1950

Early influences
Raymond (Ray) Francis Morland was born in Dunedin, a port town situated on the Otago harbour, on the east side of the South Island of New Zealand, on 23 June 1925. One of five children born to working class parents of Irish descent, Ray had four siblings: two older sisters, Margaret Mary (known as Peg), born 1918, and Eileen Patricia (Eileen), born in 1920; an older brother, William Bernard (Bill), born in 1923, and a younger brother named Kevin, who was born five years after Ray, in 1930.

Old Bill's story
Ray's father, Leo William "Bill" Morland, was born in Christchurch, New Zealand in 1880. He was the fifth child of John and Constance Morland, who had migrated at the age of 28 from Falmouth in Cornwall, England in 1863. His elder brother, Matt, was born in 1865 became the Postmaster General and lived in Wellington. His elder sister, Connie, lived in Auckland and married a lawyer. Number three was Maggie, a wealthy spinster with a shop in downtown Wellington. The fourth child was Edward, born in Christchurch who became a Transport Manager.

Completing his school education at 16, Bill realised that he was not ready to settle for a career working at some clerical job, nor was he keen to go to university. He decided that a Norwegian Whaler, getting ready to depart for the Southern Ocean, was rather more appealing. Unbeknownst to his parents, he joined the ship. After a season down in the Southern Ocean, he was still unenthusiastic about doing clerical work. This was the excuse for him to explore Australia and trek around New Zealand – no mean feat in those days!

Moving around from place to place during his travels, Bill became an expert horseman and bush carpenter (a man who can take on any kind of job, and do it well). This was fortuitous, really, as at the start of the Great War, Bill's expertise with horses was soon required to prepare horses for riders and for packs. As Ray described it, "the Government needed horses which were trained, and since Dad was one of those who 'knew' horses, he was one of the men chosen to train them."

Bill married Margaret Mary Curran in 1916. As the War progressed, the demand for horses slowed down. It was at this time that Bill made the decision to join up and serve in the army. It would have been a big decision to make since Bill and his young wife would have to face the possibility that there was no guarantee of a safe return. However, it was a decision that both Margaret and Bill did not regret making.

During his time in the army, Bill went overseas, eventually serving on the Western Front in 1917 as a signalman.

Ray tells of his father, "crawling up to the German lines and attaching his wires. Dad was a fluent Maori speaker, and this used to confuse the Germans until they found out there was a New Zealand Regiment opposite to them."

When asked if he spoke Maori, or any other languages, Ray replied that, "Dad mixed with the Maori people all of his life, so he learned Maori through that, but for myself, I don't speak any other language but Kiwi/Aussie English."

After the war, Bill returned to Otago and settled back into married life like the many other demobbed soldiers. A 'Wharfie' by this time, Bill joined the Waterside Workers Union. He also became a member of the New Zealand Labour Party, eventually becoming Spokesman for the workers and a senior official for the New Zealand Labour Party.
As Chairman of the Otago Social Policy Committee, Bill held

the weekly meeting on Sunday mornings following Mass. There were 12 members on the Committee – seven Catholics and five Orangemen. Religion was apparently never discussed as they were all far too busy planning the Social Policy programme for the 1935 Election, of which the New Zealand Labour Party won Office.

Around this time, Bill received the offer of a position in Labour politics in London, England, but he turned it down, saying "I am not in the Party for what I can get out of it for myself; I am in it for the benefit of the worker."

Ray glows with pride recalling "that was my dad, Bill Morland – a man of principle."

Bill was a man known to everybody in the Dunedin area, for offering a helping hand in times of crisis, or just by simply listening. The locals referred fondly to Bill as 'a good man' and 'you know you can always rely on Bill Morland'. What is more, according to Ray, "You could! Dad never let anybody down. He kept a promise made, and was completely loyal to Labour, and to the Union Movement."

Bill Morland was also a man completely loyal to the Crown. He had served proudly on the Western Front and because of this, made sure he attended every Dawn Parade on ANZAC Day.

A Wharfie and a man of his time, Bill was a heavy drinker. However, Ray sees it like this: "Dad was a heavy drinker, yes, but in the right place. We would see him 'merry in drink,' but never drunk. Dad was a sociable man, always with people around him, always with an opinion that counted for something."

As a child, Ray thought of his father as being a 'great bear of a man' who was always there for his children. Some years later, he described his father as "a larger than life New Zealander, who believed in the rights of the worker, the need for growth within the unions, and a man who understood the responsibilities that came with being a Labour man." It was only as he grew older, that Ray realised that the 'bear' and 'larger than life' images he held of his father as a child were less to do with Bill's physical size (actually, Bill was of slim build), but more to do with the definitive presence he felt his father had. He was certainly a man who had filled a young boy with both aspiration and admiration.

Maggie's story

Born Margaret (Maggie) Mary Curran in 1890 in Milton, New Zealand – a town around thirty miles from Dunedin, on the east coast – Ray's mother was also a person to inspire. She was the youngest of five children of an Irish farming family. Maggie was a devout Catholic, giving much of her free time to the Catholic Church.

Because of her fine soprano singing voice, Maggie soon became the voice of choice for the special Dunedin Church gatherings; she was also the person most often chosen to sing solos at the Community Concerts.

For Maggie, her greatest opportunity came when she was asked to sing a duet with the great Irish tenor, John McCormack (1884-1945). On this occasion, Maggie also sang several solos at his concert (a note of which Ray mentions later in this chapter).

A volunteer within the community as well as in the Church, Maggie was also hardworking and capable. Ray remembers her "being forever on the go! Always busy, always doing something around the house. She would be up at the crack of dawn busy cooking, cleaning, and after helping Dad with whatever meeting he was holding or attending, she would still be up at eleven o'clock at night, finishing the washing or doing the ironing."

Although only having a basic education, 'and lucky to have

that,' Maggie was a warm and compassionate woman – a woman who gave, and continued to give, until her death.

Community spirit

Maggie was also a woman on whom the Community relied heavily to help in any emergency, great or small. Ray saw his father 'as a true Jack of all trades, but a master of none.' Certainly, within their community, Bill could, and did, turn his hand to most jobs in the trades. On the other hand, Maggie was a person who seemed to know, instinctively, when a family needed help and would be there to give that help. This was not a couple who offered token gestures – this was a hard-working family, who despite not having much themselves, were still willing to share with others, and did so frequently, however small their offering.

Ray's family home was at the bottom of a hilly slope, which the older Morland children walked up daily to reach their school. During the Dunedin city flood of February 1929, the low-lying homes in the area (including Ray's) were flooded. Although the waters rose very high, Bill and Margaret managed to get the children out of the house. They took refuge with friends whose homes were higher up the hill, and thus were unaffected by the flood. They then spent the following days helping other families who were caught up in this devastating natural disaster.

Having already lived through one major flood (before Ray was born), Bill and Margaret were experienced enough to work quickly within the flooded areas and avoid the further loss of homes and belongings. They had first experienced a major flood in April 1923, when the floodwaters completely deluged Dunedin and its surrounding areas with approximately 230 millimetres of rain (all within 24 hours).

Yet, Maggie and Bill needed every ounce of strength, determination and experience to get them through the 1929 disaster. According to the 1931 report of the New Zealand

Government Documentation for Flood Hazards of Dunedin's urban streams:

"Flooding in the area of Leith was a frequent occurrence from the time of first settlement, being recorded in 1868, 1877, 1911, 1923, and 1929. The 1929 flooding being the most severe on record, with the floodwaters sweeping away bridges, and damaging other structures as well as houses. Observed flood extents, and anecdotal evidence from previous events show that inundation of (1) one metre or more occurred in some places. However, during the 1929 event, water flooded approximately five-hundred houses in the north end of Dunedin City to a depth of up to (1.2) one point two metres. (MacLean, F. W., McGregor Wilkie, J., Alexander, J. G., 1931: Water of Leith and Lindsay's Creek. Report prepared for Dunedin City Council and Otago Harbour Board, Dunedin).

Local newspapers estimated that 279 millimetres of rain had fallen in 24 hours, causing this very significant flood to occur.

Following the flood, the clean up operation took months and years, with families being temporarily re-homed until they could dry out and then repair their own homes. Some of the worst hit families needed to be completely re-homed; their own properties deemed 'beyond repair.' Although the Morland family house was badly flooded, at least, they were safe.

The images of the flood disaster, and his father's shepherding people to safety, have stayed with Ray for the last eighty-seven years, 'nudging me with the simple message of the importance of helping others.'

When asked about the ties that held his family together, Ray considered that for a moment.

"It was about family, the Community and the Parish, and the Union Movement together with the great Labour Party. With both our parents supporting us children, and each other, within those areas, the whole family felt they had a structure to work with." On family rows, Ray said, "we were a happy family. We had no fights within the family and all got along together. We may not have had much, but we did not want for anything, we were happy with what we had. We were healthy children, and I guess as all family activity revolved around the church, we all got involved."

Education – the beginning

In 1930, when he was five years old, Ray attended the St Dominic's Convent School in Dunedin. The school was run by Dominican nuns, and was about a mile and a half from their home. Ray would walk up the hill to school together with his two sisters and brother, come rain or shine. Maggie was not keen on the children having to go up the steep hill to the school at the far end of town, so she began developing a plan for a church and a school for the north end of the town, where they lived. Her plan was realised in 1932 when the Holy Name Parish was established, bringing with it the dreamed-of church, *and* the school. At the school, parents were required to assist as and when necessary. Needless to say, Ray's father came along to help. The school had quite a big playground. There were several large trees, which, with large canopies of leaves and very prominent roots, turned out to be obstacles for both the teachers and pupils alike. It was Bill who came up with the plan to fell the trees. Selling the chopped-up wood for firewood gave the School Committee a good financial start.

Ray studied at the school until 1934. It gave Ray his first encounters with people who were not white New Zealanders. "These were people," he says, "who had migrated to New Zealand. Some who had different skin colours, some with black hair, and others whose hair were more mixed browns. Some people had a fragrance around them, which smelled to me, as a very young boy, rather like exotic garlic with a mix of scented flowers – smells which I still love today."

For the five-year-old Ray, the mixing with people from diverse cultures would surely influence his future self.

Compassion, commitment and self-defence

With the four older children, Margaret stayed at home to care for them until they were all of school age. In 1931, following her decision to return to work, Margaret found work in a hotel in Dunedin. The work was mainly general household duties, which included the cleaning and washing.
Margaret would also assist in other areas of the hotel, such as the kitchen and dining room; eventually managing to persuade the hotel manager to let her take the leftover food home after work, and distribute it to families who she knew were down on their luck. Ray and his siblings frequently got the job of delivering these food parcels.

Ray recalls that, "Mum's attitude reflected that of Dad's, whose energy was focused on the unemployed worker. Their compassion and commitment to the needy were shared passions. They were parents who were always doing something to help others. An example of this is the three young men who Dad had helped during an industrial dispute. Every Sunday morning, they would deliver a forequarter of lamb to the door, which kept us in meat for five days. Another bloke, who Mum had helped out earlier with cash or food or washing, would often bring a couple of dressed rabbits round to the house, or a bucket full of whitebait..."

"These were the early experiences that I feel shaped my life. Many of the men and women, and even whole families, who Mum and Dad had helped over the years, would pay back in kind. I was always involved in some way."

This was certainly a community with spirit, pulling together in times of need. However, this is not to say that the same Community spirit was recognisable in all of the town's children.

During his early school years between the ages of five and nine, local lads had persistently bullied Ray and his young brother Kevin. Ray initially accepted it as 'par for the course' for being 'Irish Catholics in an Orange town.' This was until their father taught them to box. Ray and Kevin trained every night after school, and after that, he and Kevin were both left in relative peace.

It wasn't that the fighting stopped altogether. With the odd broken nose and missing teeth here and there, it was proof enough that the fighting continued, but possibly without the same intensity towards the Morland boys as before their boxing lessons.

Sadness and loss

In August 1938 aged only 48, Ray's mother died. Maggie had been helping to clean the Church at the end of the daily Services when she fell to the ground. Prone to high blood pressure, Maggie had suffered a devastating stroke. The ambulance took such a long time to come, that, coupled with the severity of the stroke, Maggie died in hospital just a few days later.

Maggie had been a strong influence within the family, particularly in the way she supported Bill in his work. Although Ray may have looked more to his father for advice and guidance, following the loss of his mother, there was no doubt that the household had been plunged into sadness. There must have been some quite tough moments for the family at that time, particularly for Ray and his younger brother. Yet, Ray remembers "as far as daily activities were concerned, the death of Mother did not really seem to change things, as my big sisters, Peg and Eileen, just took over the household, and life went on much as before."

Prior to her early death, all the children had been well-taught domestically by their mother, so food for the family was always properly cooked and served. Ray did the household washing on Saturdays, with the girls washing the family's clothes. From very young, and according to age and size, all the children had various household tasks to complete throughout the week. Ray quickly learned that for him, especially after Maggie's death, completing these tasks was a necessary part in maintaining the smooth running of the Morland household.

A nightingale sings

Maggie's burial took place within the Catholic Section of Anderson's Bay Cemetery. Although Ray knows he attended the funeral, he has little recollection of it. He cannot recall being at the cemetery, and has never visited her grave since. To this day, he can hear her singing – it is what he misses most about his mother.

"Mother used to sing all day long. She had a beautiful Irish soprano voice, and was a well known singer at both the Community concerts, and at the special Church Masses. When the Irish tenor and devout Catholic John McCormack visited New Zealand on one of his world tours, mother was standing beside the great man, singing solos on his stage, and singing duets with him!"

Margaret singing with the great tenor took place before Ray was born, since John McCormack gave concerts in Sydney and Melbourne in both 1911 and 1913. The tour in 1911 was headed to British Columbia, via New Zealand and Hawaii. On such stops, John McCormack would give concerts in many, smaller locations. Dates notwithstanding, Ray recounts with great pride such momentous happenings taking place within his own family, specifically, with his own beloved mother, and within the Dunedin Community.

In 1934, aged 9, Ray attended the Christian Brothers High School. As he became older, Ray became increasingly disenchanted with school; dropping out completely in the fourth form in 1939 when he was 14 years old.

"Learning to speak in a kind of French that no Frenchman would ever understand, a Latin that no one used except

Catholics – no, not for me, so I dropped out. I decided that I wanted to be a structural engineer."

When asked where he got such an idea from, Ray replied, "My own interest in this began as a ten-year old when I saw the buildings of the Post Office, and the Sydney Harbour Bridge. I saw them as magnificent structures and dreamt that I could create such marvels."

Ray also wanted other things. As he says, "I was in a dead-end job in a factory at that point, so I decided to join up (i.e. enlist in the navy). However, my big brother Bill got to hear of this and wrote to Dad to tell him not to let me join the Navy, saying it was the wrong Service for me. I realised later that he was right about that. In fact, I was just too young and although I would go regularly to the recruiting agency, none of the services would take me."

"The factory job came about because, following a school day, I would come home, stoke up the coal fire range and prepare the evening meal. I continued to do this after I had dropped out of school, without telling my dad that I wasn't in school any longer. When Dad found out, he told me to go out and get a job, so I did – in the factory!"

Did the death of his mother influence his decision to leave school? Ray thinks not.

"Education in itself was not a focus in our home. I guess in many ways we were just 'Irish labourers,' and that was our lot. However, when I was old enough to get my Apprenticeship as a boilermaker, the family thought it was great – an Apprenticeship means that Ray will be a tradesman. It was rather like my sister Peg, when she met her boyfriend, Trevor. He worked in a motorbike shop, but when war started, he joined the Air Force with the hope of becoming a mechanic, only to get himself a commission."

Events such as these were the early influences on the 'maybe I can do better' attitude he so vehemently believes in.

Although Ray might not have believed education to be an important topic in the home at that time, it certainly appeared to have been important enough for Maggie, planning as she did for a new church and school, to be built in their local area, and for Bill to continue further educating himself with his beloved politics.

Ray's father was heavily involved in the Labour Party and often out in the evenings and at weekends, attending and addressing meetings. Before she died, when Bill chaired the Community Political Rallies, Maggie would be there also with the children. They would all help prepare the supper (which was a cup of tea and a biscuit for between one and three-pence), clean up the meeting hall, and then head home.

Ray remembers his father as having "a great sense of humour, being well read in the classics, as well as being politically literate. He was one of life's characters, or a hard case, depending on how you saw him."

Maggie's death hit Bill hard. Ray said that, "although we all missed her vital presence amongst us, it was Dad who seemed to miss her steadying influence the most, both with his work and his style of living, such as getting him to limit his intake of alcohol."

"He was a workaholic and in many ways, with his own unique style of doing things. However, following Mother's death, some of Dad's amazing energy appeared to desert him and it was shortly afterwards that he seemed to withdraw from active politics."

Enlightenment and influences

Dunedin in the 1930s was a town fortunate in having, amongst others, thriving engineering and textile industries. This brought good opportunities to the area. Ray, like many young boys growing up, wanted to be many things. As mentioned, one of these was to be a structural engineer, but the advice given by his father was to apply for an apprenticeship as a boilermaker, which Ray did.

However, until he was eligible to begin this, Ray worked in a garage for eighteen months to earn himself a wage. Also, he attended night school in an attempt to raise his educational level and awareness.
At 16, he began boilermaker apprenticeship. Because of his long-held boyhood dream of becoming a structural engineer, the following years (from 1941 to 1949) were to become the most significant for Ray.

Growing up in a world of Socialist ideals, Ray regularly met up with other workers at lunchtime in the Boiler Shop where he worked. These fiery lunchtime discussions, which Ray enjoyed immensely, were about providing 'better educational opportunities for all, a better health system, with better pay and improved industrial working conditions,' although how the men thought they could meet these conditions purely by fiery discussions remains a mystery!

Ray remembers the men sitting roughly in two groups: the older, more experienced men, mainly all boilermakers, in one group, with the young apprentices (Ray included) tucked in beside them; The second group (aged between 25 to 40) were mainly welders, deemed at the time to be the 'Communist' group. Ray describes the setting: "several hardcore Communists were amongst them, with Garry and Jake having just returned home after spending four years in Spain fighting with the International Brigade. Of the others, Jack and Len, who had also just returned from Spain, were boilermakers and first-class tradesmen. They both played first-grade rugby, were members of the local branch of the Communist Party and were both Provincial representatives."

The rest of the lunchtime group were what the other men called fellow 'travellers' – they were not members of the Communist Party, but sympathetic to the Cause.

"The whole group seemed to be well-read, and appeared up-to-date with what was happening in the world. For example, they did not agree with the war, considering it to be a Capitalist ploy; however, their views seemed to change when Germany attacked Russia, they deemed it to be no longer a Capitalist ploy, but an attack on the workers, so the second group all went and 'joined up,' and all saw Service in Italy."

This was an interesting time for Ray, as a Labour-intense young man listening to various political points of view. "From extreme Socialism, to having the Communist view both vilified and embraced, without the young men seeming to know what it all stood for; it was all a very positive and enlightening experience, and it gave me great ideas for the future!"

Ray recalls sitting in on the Otago Labour Election Committee, as an eight year old.

"Dad was the Chairman, and the meeting was held at home after Sunday morning mass. In the Committee, there were 12 members (7 Catholic and 5 Orangemen). All were dedicated Socialists, there to talk, and plan the strategies for the next election. They were always planning for a 40-hour week, Social Security, free health care, pensions for all, and unemployment benefits."

Ray believes that his involvement in those early days shaped him, and says, "I am glad it did! I was able to see my father for what he was, with all his faults, and to feel lucky for the opportunity. While we were in many ways close to poverty, we felt 'really wealthy.' Yes, he was the best!"

It seems almost impossible to believe that, growing up in this completely Socialist environment, Ray would accept advice by someone outside his group, yet that is what happened. One man who was influential to Ray in other ways at that time was his hairdresser, a man named Tom. Tom had been a professional cyclist in his younger days. He was a keen fitness fan, and introduced the local young men to weight training, general fitness training, eating a balanced diet, and lastly, good personal grooming and hygiene. These were things which the young men in Ray's peer group (himself included) knew very little about.

Work, war and worries

For the first three years of his apprenticeship, Ray worked on structure. He thoroughly enjoyed everything about it, and believed that this was what he wanted to do for the rest of his working life. However, he came to realise the enormity of just what an apprenticeship meant when America became involved in World War II; the war in the Pacific brought a change in direction for all the young apprentices.

With many of the ships becoming casualties of war, Ray, who was by then halfway through his apprenticeship, found himself in one of the work gangs sent to carry out temporary repairs on these ships so they could be taken back quickly to the New Zealand docks.

Ray explains, "The ship repair gangs would be taken to the ships, by ship, wherever they were, around the different islands. Many of the ships had been torpedoed, or had other major structural damage. We would go out and do the repairs on the spot, in order to get the ships mobile enough for them to reach New Zealand for total repairs. We would work flat out for twenty, thirty, or even forty hours at a stretch if required, stopping only for coffee and food snacks. It was very tough going but that was our job. Once back in dock, we or another gang would get going again. The turn around was quick, but we must have done a good job as I used to see a fair number of ships I had worked on, some ten years later and they still looked pretty fair even then!"

In the boiler shop, because of the extreme cold, the men had big 40-gallon drums, set up as coke-burning fires. In contrast, when working on the ships, there was no warmth from a burning fire-drum – just bone-biting cold, and being continually soaked to the skin.

During the war in the Pacific Islands, the ships were many and varied. Huge ships came by carrying American Troops. Ray soon discovered the enormous differences in working conditions for the American sailors.

Compared to other ships, Ray found the living and working conditions for the American sailors were of a good standard. Clean, with good food available for all members of the crew, these ships seemed to be good places to work. On many of the other ships, Ray deemed the living and working conditions intolerable for the crews, rating the food as unpalatable, and inedible, for most of the time.

"...between June 1942 and 1944, there were between 15000, and 45000, American servicemen in the army camps in New Zealand." (Source: NZ history online. Cited: US Forces in NZ)

For the people of New Zealand, this was a revelation in itself. What with the deprivation and anxieties of war on the doorstep, together with the general and specific anxieties that come with war on the doorstep, it was a chance for them to see how the Americans lived.

Unions and decisions

After the War ended, Ray returned to his job in the boiler shop. Following his experiences on the ships however, Ray believed that Management could no longer ignore the poor working conditions of the general worker, including his own working conditions. This 'firsthand knowledge' of such diverse working conditions, resulted in Ray, with help and encouragement from his father, joining the Trade Union of Boilermakers. At the time this was happening, the Union was a strong organisation with the miners, the 'Wharfies' (and Bill as Wharfie leader), and the 'freezing' workers, setting the pace for improved working conditions in industrial New Zealand.

The latter years of the 1940s were not so kind to Ray; fired from his Boilermaker job in the Foundry, and unable to get work in other boiler shops, life was becoming quite hard. The reason for this hardship was his fight for better working conditions for all, in what was a very hard industry. As Ray explained, "I was blackballed (ostracised) by many of the heavy industrial firms who labelled me as a troublemaker, however, that was not my aim. I was just trying to change the conditions in the work environment for the better. The men were hard and the politics were hard, so I went about it the best way I could at the time."

"In total, I have been involved in the Labour and Trade Unions for 70 years in New Zealand, Canada, and Australia (in Newcastle, New South Wales for 35 years). I got my Socialist attitudes and views from my father as I was growing up, views which were reinforced by my association with my Communist mates in the boiler shop when I was 16 to 21."

Nowadays, although Ray has said he will remain a life member of the Australian Labour Party, he believes the Party has moved too far to the right, and has lost its way, as far as 'true Labour Values' are concerned.

Education – crossing the tracks

Trying to work through these difficult times appears to have been the impetus that gave Ray the opportunity to rethink his life. As a Boilermaker and a radical trade unionist assisting workers in sorting out their work disputes, large and small, had become a daily event for him. He became increasingly frustrated with his inability to get his point across to the

authorities about the poor working conditions within the industries. Ray was also beginning to realise that it was his lack of formal education which was holding him back.
"Having wanted to study a variety of subjects for some time, I just thought, why not now?"

Then, there was only one university in New Zealand – the University of New Zealand. Located in Wellington on the North Island, it was the only University qualified to award degrees. The other universities on both the North and South Islands were University Colleges, which could bestow only diplomas. However, if a student attended either Auckland or Canterbury University to read for a Bachelor of Arts, the University of New Zealand in Wellington would award the degree.

Although Ray had considered Psychology as a likely subject to study, he discovered that in order to become a practising Psychologist, he would need to study for many years. Also, there was no one actual course which would allow him to practice as a Psychologist afterwards. Following a long talk with some of his mates who were already at University about what he should read, the general consensus was that he should read for a Diploma in Physical Education. It was in March of 1949 that Ray began his studies for a Diploma in Physical Education at Otago University in Dunedin.

The University of Otago, founded in 1869, opened for students in 1871. It had as its motto, "Sapere aude" meaning "Dare to be wise." However, the Otago students had made their own motto, "Audeamus," which for them meant "let us dare," and Ray really felt that he had dared.
He had not only dared to dream, but says, "I dared to cross the tracks, in order to move away from the harsh reality of a life, which for someone like me – the child of poor Irish immigrants – would be a very hard, very physical working life. A life of working in the boiler shops, with no real educational prospects to look forward to, especially for a school dropout!"

Ray's choice of words is an interesting one. It was not just being adventurous enough to attempt something different, against the grain of his own family's predilections, or being compared to peers with similar backgrounds to his. It is as though the words shout out the passion he felt about what he wanted to do with his life – to learn and know new things! Would this dipping of the toe in the 'great ocean of education' be enough for Ray? Would it satisfy his mental roaming?

The answer is no. Raymond Francis Morland wanted more, and then some! Thus began Ray's quest for education and life-long learning.

A meeting of minds

The rationale for choosing a Physical Education course, particularly when he was not interested in becoming a teacher, was that the course would offer Ray sound skills in Statistics, while covering Tests and Measurement; Health Sciences (with Anatomy and Physiology classes carried out at the Medical School including laboratory work on donated cadavers); and Group Dynamics. There was the Physical Education part of the course which Ray enjoyed the most.

"I am a real physical type and the course suited me perfectly. It was always conducted to a high standard which was just as well as there were Olympians in the group. The Academic standard was also high as the class was very competitive. As far as I am concerned, the Physical Education Diploma course was the best move I ever made as it gave me a great base of knowledge to work with."

So enamoured was he with the prospects of his course, by working part-time, doing any jobs that were available, Ray was able to finance his own study programme. This was by no means an easy thing to achieve at that time.

Ray insists that he had 'been given his chance to get out of the Boiler Shop and into Further Education,' by Philip Ashton

Smithells, the Director of the School of Physical Education in Dunedin. Smithells, when accepting students with a trade, called them Artisans, therefore allowing them a little more respect within the academic community. It is clear that Ray himself still holds a great deal of respect for his late mentor.

Of Smithells, Ray says, "It was he who gave me an opportunity, when many others laughed at me for wanting to be educated. It was almost as though nobody wanted me to have even the smallest chance to better myself. It was certainly difficult in those early days."

"Smithells trusted his own judgement and believed that I would make it, and he was supportive of me all the way through."

Thus, Philip Ashton Smithells, renowned throughout the Physical Education world as 'PAS' (from his initials), was to become a person of note in the life of the young Morland.

Philip Ashton Smithells

Born in 1910, in Yorkshire, England, Philip Ashton Smithells (PAS) was educated at Cambridge University, where he received both a BA in English and Economics in 1932, and a MA in 1935.

Upon moving to New Zealand in 1939, PA Smithells took up the post of Superintendent of Physical Education, in the Department of Education, Otago University, which is where he and Ray met. Philip Ashton Smithells died in Wanganui, New Zealand, in 1977.

Information source: (Dennis McEldowney). 'Smithells, Philip Ashton,' from the Dictionary of New Zealand Biography. (TeAra – the Encyclopedia of New Zealand, updated 18-Feb-2014).

Debts, doubts, and new horizons

With his commencement at the School of Physical Education, and thanks to Smithells, things finally appeared to be going well for Ray.

Toward the end of his first year of studies and already getting his finances ready for his second year, Ray decided that a visit to Wellington was in order. His father suggested Ray make a house call to see his aunt (Bill's sister), who lived in the city. The aunt owned a shop and was therefore, considered quite a wealthy member of an otherwise poor family.

"On returning home after my trip, I was telling Dad how well the visit to Aunty had been going, and how we had been getting on quite well until she asked how I was paying my way through University. When I told her that I was working two part-time jobs, she appeared amazed, and quite impressed that one of Bill and Maggie's kids was doing okay. That was until I said one of my jobs was as a part-time barman at a hotel. Well, she nearly threw me out of the shop, so that was the end of that visit! Dad said, 'I should have told you she is a wouser and agin the drink.' That is fair enough I suppose, but I really wished he'd have told me before I went!"

Following the trip, daily life continued in much the same vein for Ray. He continued his studies, held down his two jobs, and balanced his meagre finances, until, in early 1950, after finishing the first year of his studies, a visit by a debt collector put paid to his ambitions.

After the 1929 flood, Ray's parents had to rent a house. The insurance company had come up with various ways to avoid paying out, and as a result, the Morlands lost the equity they had had. With the birth of Kevin in March, 1930, they had to move into a larger house leased by the Public Trust.

By 1950, only Ray and his father lived in the house since the rest had moved out and on with their lives. However, in May of that year, Ray started his full-time university studies leaving his dad to cope with most things domestic, alone. The problem was that Old Bill had assumed that Ray was continuing to pay the rent even while at university, and so a considerable debt accumulated. It transpired that Bill owed 35.00 pounds.

The Trust had issued an order to evict the occupants from their home, with immediate effect. However, a Senior Officer who was checking the accounts realised that the house tenants were the Morlands (he was a former school acquaintance of Ray's, who was impressed by Ray's athletic abilities). He decided to speak with Ray before the order was carried out; really to see if there was a way of helping the family out of their difficult position.

Having worked hard for so long, Ray had managed to save 37 pounds and 10 shillings. He had intended to use the money to cover his expenses and tuition fees for that academic year. Yet, upon hearing of the situation he felt he had no choice but to pay off the debt. It wiped out all his savings. As he could no longer support himself financially at the College, he saw no other option but to pull out of the Physical Education Diploma Course.

His mentor, Smithells, wanted him to stay on at college; even suggesting Ray just work part-time on his course. There was simply no more money to be had to support this idea, and it was a very downhearted Ray who headed home that day to try to sort out his life, once again.

When he reached home, Ray saw the headlines in one of the local newspapers saying something about 'New Zealand sending an Artillery Regiment to Korea – volunteers urgently needed for this mission.'

Ray made the decision to join the army, then and there. He rushed down to the Town Hall to sign up for Korea.

Signing up for the War effort, however, was not quite as easy as Ray had thought. On his way to the Town Hall, Ray met some tradesmen returning with disappointment etched on their faces. He learned that anyone with his trade as a Boilermaker could not join up for the war effort as they were needed on the home front.

"I doubled back home at a pace an Army Sergeant Major would have been proud of. I scrubbed my nails clean, got dressed-up, went back down to the Town Hall, and told them I was a shop assistant. I was accepted!"

"When I got back home and told Dad, who was about 70 years old then, he said that he would be sad to see me go, but was proud of me for signing on."

Chapter Two

1950 - 1980

Images of war

In June 1950 at the age of 25, Ray joined the 16th Field Regiment Royal New Zealand Army (RNZA). He undertook basic training in the South Island before completing his military training on the North Island.

He was posted out immediately after this. Following the invasion of South Korea by North Korea, Ray spent two years in South Korea, with a short spell in Manila, a former capital city lying on the east coast of the Philippines.

"I drove a truck – no drama, no heroics. I would drive my truck sometimes thirty, sometimes fifty miles back and forth to the depot to collect rations – every day. Once the rations were delivered I would be given mainly odd jobs, such as picking up wounded men and taking them to hospital; taking a twenty-five pounder gun back to the gunsmith for repairs. We did so many different kinds of jobs. Sometimes at night, a few of us would go out to secure the perimeters around the camps. It was all mundane stuff really"

Ray also had a short spell in Kure, Japan, to establish a Base Kit Store. Kure is a naval base and port for shipyards and engineering, around twenty-two miles southeast of Hiroshima on the South coast of Honshu, Japan.

It was during this two-year spell outside of his homeland that Ray witnessed, firsthand, the hardships experienced by the people of those countries, and the abject poverty in which they lived. These images have stayed with Ray his whole life.

Education and the workplace

On his return from Korea in June 1952, and having saved enough money, Ray re-entered Otago University a month later. He continued his studies and received his Diploma in Physical Education in December 1953.

Unlike his course peers, many of whom wanted to be teachers from the beginning, Ray did not wish to teach. He decided to talk things through with Smithells, who wholeheartedly agreed with Ray about the teaching situation. He suggested Ray look at welfare work, perhaps in a teenage or adult setting.

Smithells, who was not without contacts within the Correctional System, also suggested that Ray think about working in Corrections. He even called a contact of his in the Prison Service.

The contact turned out to be Sam Barnett, the Secretary for Justice, and widely regarded as *the* top civil servant – he had been tasked with 'dragging Corrections out of the 18th century.' Three days later, Ray received a letter setting up an interview with Sam, Jim Caughley, the Chief Psychologist in the Justice Department, and Lt Col Harry Blake, the superintendent of Invercargill Borstal. Ray got on well with Blake, who had commanded the 16th Field Regiment during World War II. He was offered a job on the spot.

Ray joined the Prison Service as a Borstal Officer at the end of December 1953, in the Justice Department of Invercargill Borstal. He was the first University graduate to take up such an appointment as a Correctional Officer. Ray would stay in the Department - taking study breaks in between - until 1965.

In accepting his new position, Ray had to move to Invercargill. It was a first year Physical Education student in Otago who contacted his own parents to help arrange accommodation for Ray in Invercargill, and it was the student's father, the

Principal Officer at the Borstal, who met Ray on his first morning in his new job.

First impressions

Ray was attached to a 'new arrivals' group under the control of the former Army Sergeant, Harry Blake, who was a strict disciplinarian. Ray saw him as a good man to work with and, over time, learned much from his new work colleague.

When he first arrived at the Borstal, Ray's initial reaction was 'what have I got myself into?' He recalls his first impressions of the institution and its inmates: "The inside of the building seemed to close in on me. I found the images of what I saw very hard to take in, then later, very hard to forget, particularly when seeing how the inmates behaved. Some dragged themselves around in their cells, while others appeared to be severely depressed, barely moving all day."

Being an outsider in this particular setting was not without its difficulties. Most of the staff members were long-term employees from the local area who appeared to resent any new staff members coming into the Department. Ray believed this was for two reasons; the first, that he was taking a job which they felt should be given to a local man, and second, in case he, the new staff member, wanted to change the dynamics of the place; which as it stood, gave most of the workforce, to say the least, a very easy day.

Ray was not overly concerned about any of this at the time, as he knew he had the support of the Superintendent, a former Artillery soldier, who, it turned out, knew most of the Officers from the 16th Field Regiment (Ray's former Regiment).

Old influences, new beginnings

Although Ray adjusted to his new environment and his work colleagues, he never got used to seeing the inmates just shuffling around, as though they had nothing in their lives and nothing to look forward to. As the months passed, Ray was constantly trying to think of ways in which he could help these people, rather than just maintaining the daily watch on them.

Up to that point, Ray had been a smoker. Following a particularly nasty throat infection, a visit to his doctor not only convinced him of the need to quit smoking, but also to get back the level of fitness that would help him fight further infections which were particularly rife within the work environment.

This started Ray thinking of how he could enhance the poor self-image of the inmates. He began looking at physical exercise, diet, and self-image programmes, very much as Tom Brosnan (his old hairdresser) had done with Ray and his friends by lifting their self-esteem and letting them see change was possible. The point was to let the inmates know there was another way to live their lives. Never having been a gambling man, Ray was also not much of a drinker; preferring a chocolate milk shake to alcohol (even to this day); so he was the perfect role model for many of the prisoners.

The first set of programmes Ray wrote for the young men were on social skills. The point of this was to help them become aware of personal hygiene, appearance, and relationships. As Ray says, "It was an uphill battle really. The inmates had been negatively socialised, and they would always take the easy way out, giving up as soon as a hurdle appeared."

Statistically, over ninety percent of the inmates (aged from seventeen years) had started out with Child Welfare as unruly kids. They were bullies and would be disruptive in class. The normal progression for them seemed to be to go from Child Welfare supervision to Child Welfare Group homes to Borstal. After release, they would be out for no more than six months before they were back inside again, with most of them 'doing life' in short stretches. Ray said that when he went to visit the different prisons, he would know many of the inmates.

Also, he started physical training for a rugby team within the borstal. Some of the inmates saw this as an opportunity to take on Ray, but as usual, Ray was no pushover. He defended himself well and soon won respect – to the point where there was even a demand to get into his training groups.

Sadness and success

The Prison Authorities became more and more impressed with Ray's work, both in terms of the programmes he was writing, and the positive effect these were having on the young inmates. At the beginning of 1954, while working as a Correctional Officer, the Victoria University in Wellington awarded him a Scholarship to study for a Diploma in Social Science. With relish, he embarked on the program. Typically though, as was often the case when Ray made plans, other life issues got in the way. This time, Ray's father became unwell.

Old Bill had written to Ray to say that he was going to Tauranga to stay with Ray's older sister Peg for a few weeks, after which he would visit Bill Jr, Ray's older brother, and stay with him for a while. Ray sent Bill air-tickets for the flight to Tauranga, plus some cash in case he needed a 'bit extra' for his trip.

Bill had only been in Tauranga for one day, when he became quite ill. Not knowing what the problem was, Peg phoned the doctor who immediately sent him to hospital. Although Bill rallied after a day or so, he was not keen on taking the medication doled out to him. This stubbornness only served to exacerbate his illness. One of the hospital doctors was an old Digger (like Bill) from the Great War. He knew Bill was very ill with bowel cancer and would not last much longer; therefore, he prescribed Bill a double whisky four times a day. The duty of administering this 'medicine' fell upon Peg's husband who would drop in daily and end the visit with a 'big' double scotch. It seemed to do the trick perfectly. Bill was still his own man to the end.

In November 1956, Ray travelled up to Tauranga from Wellington to visit his father for a weekend. He told Bill he would visit again the following weekend. Bill died during the following week, leaving Ray unable to say his goodbyes. This was a particularly upsetting time for Ray, as his College Exams were to be held in the same week as Bill's funeral. He made a decision not to attend the funeral but sit his Exams instead. Ray justified it as the right thing to do – knowing his father would have said, "Sit the Exams. Sit the Exams!"

From this moment on, Ray's commitment to education and everything that he had learned from his mentors began to shape his dream of helping others. It had moved on from when his parents first taught their children how to help others within the community to a more formal setting. However, Ray's parents were most certainly his first teachers.

Ray says that he often thinks how fortunate he was to have had such wonderful parents, and "while we did not get material wealth from them, we got love, security, integrity, and honesty. Yes, we were certainly fortunate in every way."

As with his mother, Ray never visited his father's grave. It wasn't until 2005, when he and his wife were at the Tauranga Cemetery for the burial of Lynn's sister that they realised that Bill's grave was quite close by. It was the first time he had actually seen it.

Saying hello to love

Ray graduated with a Diploma in Social Science from Victoria University in November 1956. He returned to the Probation Service in the Justice Department where he began putting his newfound knowledge to good use. With his common-sense approach and well-designed social programmes, he was able to help many of the young inmates.

Ray had several transfers within the Probation Service over the next few months, beginning with a transfer to Waikeria Prison as Welfare Officer, followed almost immediately with a transfer to Wellington Prison as Parole Officer in 1957.

Invercargill Borstal was bursting at the seams so the Prison Service decided to send 50 of the 'first offenders and low risk' inmates over to the Wi Tako Prison (now known as Rimutaka Prison), which had empty cells. These inmates were due for release within 8 months and it was Ray who was sent along to prepare them for this release. The Chief Psychologist, Jim Caughley, visited Wi Tako prison every Wednesday, where he spent up to 4 hours interviewing and assessing inmates.

Part of Ray's job was to select the inmates who would be seen by Caughley, and write the case summaries for him. Needless to say, Caughley was highly-impressed by the young Morland's work.

The Superintendent of Wi Tako Prison was a former pig farmer who had risen through the ranks (Wi Tako had a very large and productive pig farm). At a special Superintendent conference, the Wi Tako superintendent caught the ear of the Secretary of Justice. He was surprised at how a former pig farmer could dream up so many interesting ideas. It was Caughley who mentioned that the ideas were, in fact, Ray's, to which the Secretary of Justice retorted, "What the devil is Morland doing at that dead-end of a place? We need to use his talent more productively. Fix it!"

Two days later, the Chief Probation Officer went out to Wi Tako and told Ray that they were opening a new office in Tauranga. There were over 200 applicants for the job, but the Chief Probation Officer told Ray that the job was his, if he wanted it. Ray accepted, and was promoted to Probation Officer in Tauranga. It was here, in 1957, that Ray met his future wife, Lynn.

Lynn's story

Lynn was born in Tauranga on 25 November 1926. Tauranga was a small town in the Bay of Plenty on the North East coast of the North Island of New Zealand. Lynn was the third of four children, with her two elder sisters going into teaching like their mother, and Lynn's young brother becoming an Electrical Engineer. like his father.

As a teenager, Lynn was a keen athlete and tennis player. She had wanted to be a Physical Education teacher, but her mother vetoed that idea. Her second choice was to join the Navy and train as a wireless operator, but again Lynn's mother said no.

After much debate, Lynn's mother told her she would go to Auckland and train as a dressmaker. This in itself was not totally against Lynn's interests as she made her own clothes, and had a great interest in fashion. However, when she arrived in Auckland, Lynn decided that she was not going to be any ordinary, two-a-penny dressmaker. Instead, she would be someone that kept up with fashion properly. To do this, she went to Night School, eventually obtaining her Diploma in Fashion.

It was in Auckland that Lynn met her first husband, Arthur Blackbee. He was a carpenter, a first-class tradesman. They were married in 1949, when she was twenty-three years old. On 9 September 1950, Lynn and Arthur had their first child, a son named Stephen. Their second son, Paul, was born the following year on 13 September.

Just a few months later, Arthur became very ill and had to spend long periods in hospital, often for weeks at a time. It put a tremendous amount of strain on Lynn. Besides making the hospital visits to Arthur, she had to manage two very active toddlers, and make sure there was enough money coming into the house 'to keep the wolf from the door.' She did this by keeping the neighbourhood ladies and their families not only very well-dressed, but in the latest of fashions.

Yet, for all Lynn's excellent management and organisation skills, life was becoming just too difficult. Dressmaking late into the night while looking after her two very active boys and a sick husband was not easy. Shortly afterwards, the family doctor advised her that for the sake of her health and her children's, she should leave her husband, and allow him to be looked after by his mother. After a lot of soul-searching and discussion, Lynn and the boys returned to Tauranga to live with her parents. Lynn managed to obtain a full-time position in a fashion shop, as well as a second job ushering at the local cinema.

Now, Ray was the Local Probation Officer in Tauranga, staying with Peg, his sister. Every Sunday morning, Ray would drive Peg and her children to and from Mass. On one particular Sunday, Ray recalls, "after the Service, while I was waiting for Peg to finish her rounds of 'meet and greet,' I spotted this smart-looking lady – beautiful wavy hair, dressed to the nines in the latest fashion, with two young boys by her side; she was also doing the rounds and saying hello to her friends. As she passed by, she looked my way, smiled, and said hello. This happened every week after that. So, one Sunday I decided to see if I could get her talking. I asked her if she would like to go over to Matamata to the hot pools. She said yes, so we made arrangements and she said she would bring lunch."

"The trip to Matamata is about thirty miles over the Kaimas, and takes about an hour and a half by car. Once there, we decided to go into the water, but Stephen and Paul had never learnt to swim, so I started teaching them. We had a very enjoyable afternoon, and it soon became a regular thing on Sundays, after Church. We would also take a trip over to the Mount so the boys could go for a swim in the surf. They loved this and never wanted to leave the place."

"I had heard that Lynn was separated from her husband and seeking a divorce. She and the boys had returned to Tauranga, to where her parents still lived, and where they could help out with the boys. After our first outing, it wasn't long before we began spending quite a lot of time together."

Ray was a little concerned in the early days of his relationship with Lynn that Lynn's parents had never invited him to dinner at their home. "Eventually I was invited, and was well-received. I said little in the beginning however, as the conversation told me they were very Conservative, from a political point of view, so I would just nod and say nothing. With her parents always ranting on about 'Commies,' and me saying nothing, they questioned Lynn about this, and said that I didn't seem to have a position on politics. Lynn told them that I was a Socialist: "now you know, so what?" From then on the conversation steered well away from politics."

Ray and Lynn's relationship went from strength to strength. As Ray explained, "Lynn and I established a good relationship, and that was appreciated by all. My mother and my sisters had been good home managers and it turned out that Lynn was also good in this area. She was great company, had a great sense of humour, with a strong point of view, even if it was somewhat conservative."

Ray thinks of himself as being a bit of an 'odd bloke,' or 'a bit different,' but says, "I believe I changed for the better when I met Lynn. I often went to her parents' home for dinner, or we would always have a good picnic lunch, which Lynn would prepare. Within a few short months, my life in Tauranga had improved tremendously."

At work, Ray focused on his role as Probation Officer. He was committed to education and learning, not only for himself, but also for his colleagues. Together with this, and his work with the prisoners under his care, Ray gained recognition from his superiors who ranked him alongside the top Probation Officers in New Zealand.

Ray and Lynn's relationship was soon tested, however, when Ray received a fast track promotion to District Probation Officer in Invercargill. This meant having to leave Tauranga - and Lynn. Although Ray did not want to leave her, he was

Ray Morland in Pictures

N.B. Very few photographs of Ray in his earlier years exist, so most of the photographs come from the archives of Warnborough College and span the last twenty years of his association.

1949: The young Ray Morland cheekily turns his head (last row, second from right). Philip A Smithells (PAS), who influenced him so much, sits in the middle of the first row.

Philip Smithells (middle) leads the entire Diploma in Physical Education, Sport and Exercise Sciences cohort (1949-51) at the University of Otago. Ray folds his arms in the front row.

Dr Ray Morland meets the Chief of Police in Thailand and presents him with a Warnborough tie (Bangkok, 2000)

Ray (front row, left) sits with other attendees at Warnborough's Senate meeting in Malaysia (Kuala Lumpur, 2002)

Ray addresses delegates at Warnborough's 30th anniversary Senate meeting (London, 2003)

With shipping magnate, Lee Yew Kim, and Dr Brenden Tempest-Mogg (Malaysia, 2005)

Ray and Lynn with Dr Vibart Wills and Dr P Poobalan in Canterbury (UK, 2005)

With his lifelong friend George Cooper and Canon Dr Richard Martin (Australia, 2006)

With Sr Remy Junio, St Paul University President during SPU's centenary (Philippines, 2007)

At Cr Robert Wilson's (second from left) convocation with Trixie, Baroness Gardner of Parkes (third left) in Canterbury Cathedral (UK, 2007)

With key members of the Warnborough 'family' in front of Canterbury Cathedral (UK, 2006)

At his student Robert Isaacs' convocation (UK, 2013)

In Parkes, NSW where Dr Ian Cooper presented the results of his PhD research into Parkinson's Disease. The late Mayor of Parkes, Cr Robert Wilson, had supported this project through Ray's initiative and a full scholarship from Warnborough College (Australia, 2009)

With key Warnborough members at a meeting (Hong Kong, 2008)

Ray and Lynn enjoying a light moment (Australia, 2006)

The family including stepsons Stephen and Paul celebrating Lynn's 80th birthday (Australia, 2006)

The happy couple in Newcastle (Australia, 2015)

advised by colleagues to accept the promotion or it could have an adverse affect on his future prospects. Fearing he would become lost in the system if he turned down the appointment, Ray moved back to Invercargill with a very heavy heart indeed.

Ships, drugs and the nuns' chorus

As the new District Probation Officer in Invercargill, Ray had to establish a new District. This kept him busy, which had the added benefit of helping him to get over, in part anyway, his separation from Lynn.

Meeting prisoners with addictions was very frustrating for Ray. It was a constant battle of attempting to understand them on the one hand, and trying to give help with the other. The majority of the inmates in the borstal system were drug addicts. A large proportion of these could either be extremely violent or very withdrawn; both of which were extreme behaviours.

Such was his commitment to helping people in need, as in this case his charges in the prison system, and realising that he did not know enough about drug addicts, and the behaviours associated with addictions, Ray decided that further studies were necessary. After over a year in Invercargill, and corresponding with friends who were studying overseas, Ray realised that perhaps it was time to upgrade his own academic qualifications.

Lynn was not happy about this decision, but Ray's need to study overseas was, for him, all compelling. In March 1960, Ray obtained permission to take unpaid leave for one year in order to travel to Canada. For Ray, furthering his education meant helping others in a more professional way. (Looking back on this experience now, Ray believes that he made a big mistake, and that he should have applied for funding, and then secured the courses, rather than rushing off without putting an appropriate plan in place).

He secured a working passage to Canada with a large export company transporting frozen meats to the United Kingdom and America. He took his place on the Port Victor, a British freighter.

"The ship left Auckland and headed to America via the Panama Canal, then further up the coast, stopping in New York, before heading out to Montreal."

During his short stint in New York, Ray visited the Social Welfare Agencies who dealt with the drug dealers and addicts, recalling also, his visit to Sing Sing, the famous Correctional Facility. "I viewed the bone-chillingly cold, and clinical, death chamber, and sat in the electric chair. The whole Prison was more than just a cold and uninviting place, it was soul-destroying!"

En route to Montreal, Ray decided to leave the ship in Toronto. It was July 1960. He had wanted to study about drug addiction. Vancouver on the west coast of Canada was the main port where all the drugs came in from the Far East. That was the place to be, so he hopped onto a Greyhound bus and crossed the country.

On his arrival in Vancouver, he booked himself into the local YMCA. Ray then successfully applied to the Western Washington State College for a BA and a Master's Degree, with the working Practicum for this course being held at the Catholic Children's Aid Society in Vancouver.

The Provincial Government for Child Welfare was purely administrative at that time, with authority delegated out to private agencies, such as the Catholic Society, the Jewish Agency, the Salvation Army, and others. The ages of the placed children ranged from birth up to twenty-one years, giving the carers some difficult challenges along the way. This proved an interesting place to become involved with, for more than one reason.

Ray was a champion boxer, thanks in part to the boxing lessons his father had given him as a child, to avoid being 'thrashed' by the local bullies at school. During his army years, he had completed a Commando course as a British Army Combat specialist. These were skills much appreciated by the nuns when Ray, together with other members of the Society, went out at night to try to rescue children who were being 'used' by the drug gangs.

There were times when his group was faced with 'some very angry and disturbed' people. In Ray's succinct words: "What would you do if a drink-crazy bloke came at you demanding money for drugs, swinging a broken bottle in his fist, ready to smash it into your face? Would you approach the man as the nuns do and sing, or as the psychologists told us to, and say to the men, 'Why are you angry, young man? Come, let us talk about it.' Or, would you use my idea of *direct therapy* in these situations, and use a right cross and a left hook?"

Sometimes, the latter method was necessary. The group was often successful during these midnight escapades, saving both, the lives and the futures, of many young children and teenagers, and, of course, the nuns!

Mates, marches, memories and marriage

Ray was able to complete his BA at Western Washington State College in Bellingham. He achieved this with the help of his advanced standing, studying part time and attending Summer Schools. To finance his studies and complete his Practicum, Ray needed to find a job, and soon. Hearing on the grapevine that there could be something at Western, he applied for, and got, the job of coach to the College Rugby Team. The pay was good, and it was only sixty miles to Bellingham from Vancouver, where he lived.

In Vancouver, Ray met up with an old friend from Otago University, John Drinkwater (a plumber by trade) and another of PAS's artisans. John had been a year behind Ray in their

Physical Education studies in Otago. As a champion swimmer, he was upgrading his Diploma of Physical Education to a Bachelor Degree in Physical Education. Apart from their courses, both men shared a similar passion: they were 'mad about bands.'

"Some Sunday evenings, after tea, we would go down to the town square and listen to the Salvation Army band conduct a Service. We both just loved the music and the singing, and after the service, the band would line up ready to march up to the Citadel, where there would be a free meal for the needy. John and I would line up, alongside the homeless and the poor, and when the bandmaster called 'by the centre quick march,' the band would strike up, playing 'Marching to Glory,' and we would all march the mile back to the Citadel, singing and laughing. As the Salvation Army never turned anybody away from their door, everyone present would be invited in for a meal and a chat afterwards. It was a real thrill. Ah, memories! Yes, those were indeed happy times!"

For many years afterwards, whenever they met up, John and Ray would look back fondly on those days.

Music brought back memories for Ray of a time when, aged five, he went shopping in Dunedin with his mother. They had watched a brass band playing in the town centre. Ray could remember a man, smoking a cigar, who was also watching the band – he had put the two together (the brass band and the smell of the cigar), and called it a 'baccy band.' Ray thinks of this as being one of his earliest recollections of image association.

Upon finishing his Practicum, Ray had to begin studying full time for his Master's degree in Education (M. Ed). He managed to obtain a further twelve months study leave without pay from Invercargill, although the department was none too happy about this.

“I was missing Lynn a lot. And, with the prospect of a further year without her, I decided to take the plunge and ask Lynn to marry me. Lynn said ‘yes’ and proceeded to join me in Vancouver with her two boys, who were 12 and 11 years old at the time. It was really a smart thing that I did back then.”

Lynn and the boys landed in Vancouver on 31 October 1962, and she and Ray were married on that day with Ray’s colleague Stan, and his wife Val, as witnesses. Ray and his new family left for Bellingham the following day.

Ray had arranged for campus housing and bought some necessary furniture. The accommodation was a ‘no frills house’ with rent set at 20 US dollars a week. Lynn did not complain. On the contrary, she made it into a very smart and comfortable home. The boys soon became the centre of attention in their Middle school, with their New Zealand accent.

“Once Lynn came into my life it changed for the better; in many ways, meeting Lynn seems to have been what I was waiting for,” says Ray.

After someone suggested that the Morland family invest in some American-style clothes (namely, long trousers), Lynn paid a visit to the fashion department in one of the large stores. She recalls the store as being ‘a bit chaotic.’ She was almost sorting out the department for them when she was offered a full-time position in fashion sales by the store manager, who was very interested in Lynn’s approach to fashion and design. As she did not have a work visa, Lynn had no option but to turn the offer down. In their circle of friends, many of the wives worked whilst their husbands studied. By becoming their regular babysitter, Lynn was thus able to supplement the family income in this way.

An interesting aside which Lynn only found out upon their return to New Zealand: her grandfather was actually American (born in New York).So, it was a possibility that she may have been eligible for a work visa after all.

"During that time in Washington, we lived on 'specials.' Our main meals came from hamburger mince. Lynn used this in three ways: stewed, curried, and in a pie. We also bought frozen meals when they were on special offer. One of my student colleagues used to invite himself to dinner when a pie was on the menu. He considered Lynn's meat pie as a 'really special' event. He was not a poor student. He was an ex-Naval Officer, who taught at a Seattle high school. The good thing was he would always arrive with the dessert and extras. Also, I remember the campus caretaker, a young American Air Force Officer on leave, who would bring Lynn a fresh salmon when in season. He would show her how to cook it. He retired from the American Air Force as a Colonel, and still keeps in touch with us - even after 54 years!"

Paul and Stephen really enjoyed their stay at the local school and took advantage of the many activities available to them. Lynn, too, was making her own friends, and helping Ray by editing his assignment papers.

Relocation and recognition

On finishing his Master's Degree, Ray looked at other courses which had scholarships attached to them with multinational firms. He sent an application to Princeton University, who had an interesting course in Human Resources (HR).

It turned out that they also had an interest in Ray. However, after working out the logistics, Ray decided not to follow up on his application but to head back to New Zealand instead. Lynn packed the family belongings and they all headed back to Vancouver to wait for the ship to take them home.

One deciding factor in taking this decision was Lynn's ongoing health issues. Lynn and Ray had a fear of incurring high medical costs in America. At the time, they both considered it to be a wise move. Even now, after many years, they have no regrets.

"In Vancouver, we had to wait a few weeks for the ship home. We rented an apartment close to King's Park, where the boys would go to feed the chipmunks. We travelled home on the Oriana, which was a very different ship to the one I initially sailed into Vancouver on," said Ray.

Within a day or two of docking in Auckland, Ray went down to Wellington to report to back to Headquarters and to get back onto the payroll.

All this while, he had not seen much of his good friend and supporter, Jim Caughley, the Chief Psychologist. However, when Caughley heard that Ray had returned (with a Master's degree), he had Ray seconded to the Psychological Services department at the Waikeria Correctional Centre, to establish the Group Counselling Programme. This did not appear too bad as he, Lynn and the boys would get a house in the Staff Village. However, it was yet another move for Lynn, and one which would be rather isolating as Ray did not have a car – at that time cars were hard to get due to the restriction on overseas funds. Nonetheless, that did not deter Lynn, with her ever sunny disposition. She soon settled her family in and made a home in the village.

It was not plain sailing in Waikeria for Ray.

"There was no easy transition for us in the village, as there was a definite 'them and us' attitude between the Prison Officers wives, and the professional staff. It was also hard-going trying to get something new started in the workplace, as a certain section of staff appeared to think I was trying to take over their jobs. This was far from the truth, but as it became more and more difficult, I reported back to Jim Caughley and told him that I wanted to go back to the Probation Service."

In 1963, Ray was offered the job of District Probation Officer in Paeroa, to establish a new office in the Thames District of North Waikato. This meant yet another move for the family and new schools for the boys. Although the boys missed the superb facilities they had experienced in the American schools, for Lynn, it was only a two to three-hour drive to Tauranga to her parents.

Ray remained in Paeroa until early 1965, when he felt that he had exhausted all future possibilities for advancement in the Probation Service. There were no other promotions available, or possible, in the areas that he interest in working.

Wanting to get value for his Masters degree, Ray applied to be the Staff Training Officer in Wellington. He was successful in his application. Transferring to the State Services Commission meant yet another house move, and another new school for Stephen and Paul.

Ray remembers the move as "going quite well. We built a very acceptable Cape Cod model house in Tawa, about twenty miles from Wellington, which was just thirty minutes by rail. We had to get a second mortgage to finance our new home as I had 'missed out' on obtaining a Rehabilitation Loan because my availability had expired. Lynn secured a position in fashion at a large department store, and the boys enrolled at Wellington College. This is it, we thought, no more moves."

After only two years, Ray was again looking for advancement in his career but "it was not on the Department's agenda. So, I started to look for an academic position and saw one in Perth, Australia. I applied, and was successful. Although we had said 'no more house moves', and this would be one of the biggest moves we would make as a family, we all looked forward to moving to Australia. Perth was renowned as a beautiful city."

In early 1968, the family made their move. With Lynn in charge of designing their new house for the plot of land that they had purchased, and the boys relishing their new school and country, Ray began his new appointment as a lecturer in the Department of Social Work, at the Western Australia Institute of Technology (WAIT).

The degree courses at WAIT were four-year courses, and initially, Ray taught Social Issues, and Social Administration. While it was comparatively easy for a white Australian to gain entry onto a university course, for the indigenous groups, it proved anything but easy. This was a detail recognised by Ray immediately.

Ray recalls thinking that, "when it came to education and the Aborigines, I felt there was a need to address at least some of their issues; like many teenagers who may have been rebellious, or messed up in school, they might now be rueing their lost opportunities. I thought that a 'second chance' at education might well be the answer.

I knew that the State Health Department was intending to appoint several Aboriginals to the positions of Liaison Officer, but I also knew that these new recruits would not be given the training they required to actually do the job. It would simply be setting these people up for failure."

Ray decided on a plan of action. Once he had his plan worked out, Ray approached Eric Atkinson, the Head of the Department for Psychology and Social Work in WAIT, seeking approval to develop short courses aimed at the indigenous people. The aim was to help them learn some skills, while bringing in visiting guest speakers to inspire the students. Eric threw his support behind both ideas immediately. With Ray writing the courses, they successfully applied for funds from the Department of Aboriginal Affairs.

The courses were an immediate success, with the students making the most of the new opportunities as Ray had predicted. However, after a while, the indigenous students wanted more. Thereafter, on the back of a visit by the Aboriginal Elders, Ray wrote several new programmes – some for one-day seminars, and others, which became known as bridging courses to facilitate entry into higher education or to getting a job in local Government or manufacturing.

The bridging course was a six-month full-time course, requiring about ten hours of attendance per week. Ray recruited two of his graduates who had worked in Aboriginal Affairs as field officers, and a very experienced teacher of English who had taught English to Asian government officers. As such, the bridging courses took off and became very successful. At the end of the courses, there would be a Graduation Ceremony, with all the staff wearing their robes and the Certificates being handed out by the Director.

Pride and prejudice

Ray continued to work hard with the students and was promoted to Senior Lecturer in 1972. He received accolades for the great success of his courses and seminars.

"The only sour note was that in many instances, the social workers refused to supervise our students during their Practicum. Two colleagues and I had to set up our own groups in agencies that would accommodate us. After three years, we had graduates out in the field ready to get on with the job. They soon made their mark as competent professionals, and began to take on the role of supervisors."

One of the courses Ray initiated was a training programme in Aboriginal Affairs. Robert Isaacs, an Aboriginal Elder, was one of the first students to participate in the programme. Ray was particularly proud of Robert. Following his initial successes in his studies, Robert went on to achieve much more, while picking up the reins of Ray's work (that of bridging the cultural divide between Aboriginal people and government processes). Robert was elected Deputy Mayor for the city of Gosnells.

Robert's wife had been a student, too, on some of Ray's courses. She had become a friend of Ray and Lynn's. She, like most of the others, saw the courses as lifelines – not only helping to ensure a future for themselves, but also for their children.

One Aboriginal student was a young man, married, with two small children, living in a house shared with three other couples, all with children.

"After the evening meal, the young man would put the kids to bed and he would take his books and go down the street to the pole with a light, and that is where he studied, if it rained, he would simply use an umbrella. He passed his courses, and eventually got his Diploma, which helped him to get a job, and a house, now that he could pay the rent. Along with that, now that the young man had an address, the Health Nurse could call and check on the kids. The vicious cycle that he was in was broken.

This is what started me on what I called the 'Total Approach.' You do not look at one thing you need to look at the whole cycle – Education, Work, Accommodation and Health."

"I look at it this way: 'education is being able to teach the next generation.' For example, many of the children of the first set of students went on to higher education, with some becoming medical doctors, accountants, lawyers, teachers, and engineers. Therefore, it is highly likely that their children will eventually move towards higher education. I felt proud of the fact that with Eric at the helm, we had, what I thought, was a good working team."

Sadly, this was not to last. Towards the end of 1978, Eric Atkinson had a stroke. Ray and Lynn were both shocked by this event, but there was worse to come. A few months later, Eric died, in his mid-fifties, without ever returning to work. It was the turning point for rapid change within the Department. Ray's hard political stance on many of the daily issues associated with teaching was becoming less and less popular. Many of the University members wanted him removed from office. There were many purported reasons for the Department taking this stand, one being that not everyone accepted what was regarded as Ray's 'foreign' qualifications, or his appointment as Senior Lecturer. All this upset in the workplace caused turmoil in Ray's life on a day-to-day basis.

"On one occasion, one of my students – a farmer's daughter, very conservative, right wing, and not very bright – had complained to the authorities that I was teaching socialism. There was 'heck to pay.' The governors rifled through my notes and questioned other students who told them that I was teaching socialisation, not socialism. It did not matter. Mud sticks!"

Ray had been writing and coordinating several courses on Alcohol Abuse for Aboriginal Community Workers, courses which other staff members tried to stop. In spite of these difficulties, Ray soldiered on to help the indigenous groups by attending meetings, writing new programmes, and creating new groups of students.

One of these meetings finished very late in the evening, making it necessary for Ray to stay overnight in a hotel due to the distance between the venue and his home. However, after a restless couple of hours trying to sleep, Ray decided to drive home, arriving just before 5 in the morning. He found that a message had been delivered to the house late the night before, informing him of a very important meeting which he was to attend, which would be taking place at 0800 hours, that same day.

Needless to say, he turned up at the meeting. He noted that although many people were present, the meeting itself addressed nothing of any importance. However, his presence there had apparently surprised quite a few people. It was only then that Ray realised he was not expected to have made it to the meeting in time, giving more ammunition to the 'anti-Ray brigade.'

Ray found the whole affair very sordid and petty. "At that meeting, my look of contempt probably said it all."

The unpleasantness and dark times continued. There were upsets occurring on a daily basis, which was hardly good for his own morale, let alone the students', who became involved by default. Unable to oust him from the Department because he had managed to attend the meeting, it seemed his detractors had decided to raise the stakes.

The main incident that Ray describes, here, completely shattered him and turned his life upside down forever.

"It started like this. Administration said I had stolen $5000 from WAIT Aid. WAIT Aid, who ran my Aboriginal Courses, had posted a cheque to my home address. This was for $5000, made out in my name and crossed 'Not Negotiable.' I was never paid by personal cheque anyway and being busy at the time, I must have waited about 3 weeks, and receiving no call to say it was a mistake, I went to WAIT Aid, and spoke to the Manager who had signed the Cheque. The Manager said just to cash it as it was for me, so I did."

Ray believes there had been supposition of direct political interference from outside factors, due to unrest about mining and land rights with the indigenous people, which, throughout the years, had been an ongoing concern. This of course, is not a confirmed fact but as far as Ray is concerned, it is still a possibility.

"It was shortly after that when Administration told me that by cashing the cheque I had stolen the money. I was completely devastated by this accusation. I felt that I could not take in enough air to keep my body upright. I suppose now, it would be described as me having a panic attack, such was the effect on me! I was given the choice of one of two solutions to the problem: I could be sacked, with the possibility of it becoming public, with the humiliation which follows such a thing like that, and the human thinking, a sort of 'no smoke without fire,' or I could resign, with immediate effect."

"A short time later when the Auditors were called in to check everything out, they found that WAIT Aid actually owed me $15000!"

Even so, Ray says that it was all quite irrelevant; with Eric's death, and with no one left in authority willing to support him, he resigned from WAIT in 1980.

Vindication

Ray recalled visiting Perth some three years later. He had phoned the Director at WAIT, who told him that 'it' should never have happened.

Regardless, Ray was unable to get his question of just why it did happen, answered.

"I regret that I did not go to the police and sue WAIT and WAIT Aid and all the others concerned. I would still like to know who so badly wanted me out at that time, and why, whoever they were, or are, they would go to such lengths to try to achieve this. I guess I never will find out their reasons now, as most of the key players are dead!"

Ray bristles with pride when he recalls a senior official in Federal Health saying that he considered Ray's work with the Aboriginal People to be the only significant contribution for

Aboriginal advancement. Following the success of the programmes, in 1982, the Federal Government gave WAIT/Curtin University 8 million dollars to build a permanent Aboriginal Enclave on campus.

"Although this happened after I had left WAIT, it came about because of my early work in getting the Aboriginal communities involved in education; something which I had been working on for some time, so what started in the 1970s, became fact in 1982."

In early 1987, WAIT became Curtin University of Technology.

Chapter Three
1980 – 2000

The pinnacle

During his latter years at WAIT, Ray began studying for a PhD at nearby Murdoch University; writing on the subject of how to prevent alcohol abuse in Aboriginals. This proved a difficult subject to research, as talks with the Elders, although necessary, were fraught with cultural correctness. As Ray explained, "First, one had to apply and then wait for an invitation into the camp – no mean feat to begin with. This process could take many months, with sometimes an invite being issued, and at other times, no invite."

In order to not waste time, Ray had started reviewing the small amount of literature he had managed to collect up to that point. However, with Murdoch University continuing to ask for progress reports on his work, and Ray not being able to show any progress, he felt obliged to leave the course.

Following his resignation from WAIT in June 1980, Ray went into a slump. He felt angry and confused about how WAIT had treated him, but knew he had no way of changing that. He was jobless, yet needed to provide for his family, and he still had within him an almost burning desire to help the indigenous students. All of these things, he knew, needed to be addressed. More importantly, Ray felt he needed to prove to himself that he had 'got things right.'

Priorities first, Ray decided to focus on completing his PhD. This he did with remarkable speed, a lot of hard work, and, with an element of good luck. This 'bit of luck' came in the shape of an invitation to attend a World Health Organisation Workshop in Edinburgh, Scotland.

As one does at such events, Ray met several people, who as a group, got on well with each other immediately. One member of the group was Dr Ben Blake, an American from the US Federal Department of Health. He spent several hours discussing Ray's intended dissertation which was focused on strategies to reduce alcohol abuse in the Aboriginal population, amongst other similar issues.

Following the general exchange of work and contact details, as happens before leaving most Conferences and Workshops, the American said 'to ring him,' should Ray need any information on the health issues relevant to their discussions.

Graft and gratitude

After returning home and picking up where he left off, Ray realised there was not a great deal of reference material available to him for his research. In desperate need of some validation for the statistics in his work, he gave the American a call. Three weeks later, a very large parcel arrived for from his new friend, containing over two hundred summaries of articles on the subject of alcohol abuse in indigenous peoples.

To say Ray was grateful for the information received would be an understatement; he was simply ecstatic. With several years of research already 'under his belt,' he wasted no more time and began writing up his notes and validating his own findings using the data sent from America. By working long into the night, Ray was able to complete his Doctoral dissertation in less than six months since resigning his position at WAIT. This of course was not the end of the matter.

A degree of recognition

Ray had to find a university which would give him full accreditation for his work. Resourceful as ever, he turned to yet another American: Dr Aaron Bindman. Dr Bindman had been one of his visiting American professors in WAIT. In fact, Dr Bindman had completed a review of the development of enclaves in Australia for WAIT and he strongly endorsed Ray's work, believing the courses to be highly effective. He recommended that Ray enrol at the Union Institute in Ohio, America. The reason for this was that unlike most other universities, the Union Institute did not require students to do course work.

Ray flew to Cincinnati for an interview, and the Institute spent three hours reviewing his curriculum vitae and the PhD work he had done at Murdoch University, and asking about his educational philosophy.

Impressed with him, the Institute awarded him advanced standing, which reduced his total time on the program to only two years. Nonetheless, he was still compelled to attend some seminars in Ohio, and would eventually face a dissertation panel in New York. His main supervisor was a man called Dr Marvin Surkin, who also became a good friend.

Ray found these events most enjoyable as he felt the other students were, as he says, "a bit like me – rejects from other universities. They were capable, creative individuals, who worked outside of the square; people who worked as psychiatrists, teachers, health workers including medical doctors. There were also men and women from all sorts of agencies, who worked in the area of alcohol abuse, which stirred my interests greatly."

Although this amount of travelling added to the cost, Lynn accompanied Ray on this trip. They both looked upon this time away, not simply as study time, but also as a holiday, enjoying both the company of the people they met along the way, and the experience of being in the country itself. Finally, at the end of 1980, graduating with the title 'Doctor' after his name, it was time for Ray and Lynn to return home, and for Ray to look for a job.

Search and rescue

It took Ray several months of intensive search to find work, but towards the end of the Australian summer of 1981, he accepted an appointment as the Head of Department of Social Administration at the Newcastle College of Advanced Education. *This meant yet another move for the Morland family.*

Like many cities in the world, Newcastle was not a place to forge new and lasting friendships. Even the boys' friends were limited to their classmates, and although Lynn had built up a small circle of friends with whom she would meet every so often, the Morlands found Newcastle to be quite a lonely experience. Indomitable to the end, they persevered to make good on their new life.

Their good friends from Perth (and fellow advocates for indigenous peoples rights), David and Betsy Buchanan, flew over for dinner every now and then. They, plus a few other close friends made life bearable, even happy. Lynn's great cooking skills ensured that their dinner parties were fun-filled (and tummy-filling) occasions.

Two-year Associate Diploma courses were offered in Newcastle. For these, Ray taught the same courses as he did in WAIT, but with a slightly different slant in order to accommodate the shorter learning times available to the students.

As he had done in WAIT, Ray came to the rescue of many budding students, young and old, who had failed the initial entrance test for the social work course. These people came from all walks of life, including reformed alcoholics, 'battered wives', former drug addicts, and even a failed bank robber!

Variety notwithstanding, Ray said, "I was able to give them all a go, and they all made the most of the opportunity."

In 1987, Newcastle University took over the running of the Newcastle College for Advanced Education. Ray became a Senior Lecturer in the School of Administration and Technology, and continued to run his various courses until retiring in 1990 at the age of sixty-five.

This was an enforced retirement for Ray. He would have enjoyed teaching for a few more years: quite the opposite of his initial feelings on teaching. However, Newcastle University's rules on retirement required members of staff to finish the year out on reaching retirement age, and then leave. As his birthday fell mid-year, Ray was given a six-month reprieve to finish work at the end of December, 1990.

End of an era

In 1991, Ray became a Retirement Consultant. One of Ray's former students who was involved in the development of a retirement village had asked Ray to speak to groups of business people involved in the project on the subject of 'The Needs of the Elderly.' This led to Ray's election to the New South Wales Council for the Elderly, which meant monthly meeting trips to Sydney.

According to Ray, "it was a very conservative group, with the building of retirement villages, and rest homes being all the rage at the time, and with government monies available to spend, the developers were all very keen to be involved!"

It didn't take long for Ray to realise that his socialist views of wanting good standards, maintaining those standards, and making all business transactions transparent, were not compatible with the views of other group members.

"I was a thorn in their sides. I never did find out whether this was a personal snub to me or not, but the Government reformed the group into a Sydney-based one, therefore, excluding me completely from the circle."

Again, Ray recalled similar feelings to the ones he had felt when forced to leave WAIT.

The setback with the Elderly Council group did not weigh him down for long. Ray continued to help individuals, both younger and older, by trying to set up a committee and get local businesses involved. Many of the students at Newcastle University had good family business connections – this could have created many opportunities for all involved. It occurred to Ray that while Australians were scrambling to make business connections in Asia, they were ignoring one of their most valuable and most accessible entry points – overseas students - all the 'junior officers' of captains of industry, who were right on their doorstep. It was through his connections with these students that he began to build his own network of contacts in Asia, which had grown enormously in the eight years since he formed Overseas Business Education Contacts (OBEC) with a business partner, Bill Rak.

OBEC was designed as a non-profit organisation whose philosophy was all about connecting overseas students with Australian businesses. Its first big venture was in Indonesia, where Ray and Bill used their connections to help develop a multi-million dollar deal for a local company.

Once again, it proved to be another letdown for Ray. He felt the local businesses were too short-sighted and could not see the value in creating such relationships. Although he worked very hard to bring people together, the new venture eventually failed.

"For someone who has worked so hard trying to achieve goals, both for myself and others, accepting defeat has never been an easy task for me. I believed that life for all could be improved, simply by making an investment, and using some good old fashioned common sense!" says Ray.

Widening Horizons

Despite this, new beginnings were on the horizon for Ray. While on the Faculty at the University of Newcastle, he became President of the Hunter Committee for Overseas Students and was on the Board of the Academic Structures Committee.

It was Ray's job to look after the welfare of the wealthier students, who had come predominantly from southeast Asia. He wanted to look at ways of expanding opportunities for these students. In the first instance, it was to give them advancement possibilities for their studies – perhaps through graduate studies. Another idea was to cultivate a wider networking opportunity outside of Australia.

In the late 1990s, Ray came across a British college which was making waves with its then daring and pioneering methods of distance education, and which had built up a network of partnerships across southeast Asia.

The college had an Australian partner at that time, which was also based in Newcastle. The Australian partner had a connection with the University of Newcastle, which is how Ray learned of them, and then of Warnborough College. He decided to telephone Warnborough to see if any cooperation could be engendered. He spoke to then Director of Admissions, Julian Ng, and found that there were many congruent ideas between the college's philosophy and his. The conversation led to others, and soon, he was corresponding directly with Dr Brenden Tempest-Mogg, the president of Warnborough College.

Chapter Four
2000 to date

Retiring or Re-firing?

Warnborough College, headquartered in England, was a pioneer in distance learning at the time. Ray had seen that the College was already well-established in southeast Asia, with multiple partnerships across a range of countries. The idea of multinational partnerships intrigued him and his mind dreamt up many ideas for tapping into this network.

When Dr Tempest-Mogg visited the partner institution in Newcastle in 1999, it proved to be a fortuitous event for Ray. He met with Dr Tempest-Mogg, and it was a meeting of minds. Ideas flowed fast and furiously between the two educators. In 2001, Ray accepted an appointment to become Secretary to the Warnborough College Council, in Canterbury, England. It renewed his academic interest and gave him a new lease of life. He was also charged with helping to develop the curriculum for a revised Australian Studies program for Warnborough, and to advise on continuing education for mature adults from overseas to participate in workshops and study tours in Australia.

He made plans to attend the first ever Senate meeting of the College on 20 September 2001. No one had expected the terrible and tragic events that happened in New York only 9 days earlier. Despite the chaos and the travel bans, twenty key people from around the world turned up. Ray was in his element, tirelessly networking with everyone.

From that point, Ray became a very active member of the Warnborough Council, travelling to various countries within the College's partnership network to attend meetings or graduations. In 2002, he attended a Senate workshop in Kuala Lumpur and a graduation organised by Institut Teknologi

Klang (a learning centre of Warnborough College's). Here, he got to meet local dignitaries and politicians, as well as talented and successful graduates.

In 2003, he was back in the UK to help celebrate Warnborough's 30th anniversary with a graduation and a special tea at the Houses of Parliament, hosted by Sir Sydney Chapman (a Member of Parliament and a Peer). The events brought together heads of Learning Centres, students, graduates, alumni and friends from around the world, and culminated with an Elizabethan banquet at Hatfield House (Queen Elizabeth I's former palace).

Ray could see that by associating himself with a forward-thinking institution such as Warnborough, he could create and provide opportunities to its constituents; inspiring people and creating action are a big part of education, and Ray recognised these strengths in the Warnborough philosophy.

Over the years, Ray travelled from Newcastle, Australia to the Philippines, Thailand, Malaysia, the USA and the United Kingdom.

In 2005, he nominated his good friend, Betsy Ann Buchanan, for a Honoris Causa Doctorate, for all the work she had done for the indigenous peoples of Western Australia, particularly the Noongar tribe. Betsy is credited with having established Western Australia's first Community Law Centre in 1976. Now, there are 280 such centres in Western Australia. She worked as an advocate based at the Aboriginal Medical Service (later the Derbarl Yerrigan Health Service) working on cases involving housing evictions, the handicapped child's allowance, the reporting of child sexual abuse and the Royal Commission into Deaths in Custody. Her work with the Aboriginal community has spanned over 40 years. As such, Betsy was a worthy recipient of the Honoris Causa.

He campaigned for and received a full Warnborough scholarship for Ian, the son of his good friend George 'Geo' Cooper, to do an extensive study into the devastating effects of Parkinson's Disease for his PhD. Dr Ian Cooper eventually presented the fruits of his research to the city of Parkes to critical and personal acclaim in 2009.

Parkes was a small town in western New South Wales. Yet, it had a startlingly high number of sufferers of Parkinson's Disease (PD). The Mayor of Parkes at the time was Councillor Robert Wilson, OAM. He was a tireless campaigner for the rights of PD sufferers and their access to care. He afforded all assistance towards Dr Cooper's research into PD and approved schemes which could assist and alleviate the sufferings of those afflicted with PD.

Ray has been a tireless advocate of new partnerships, often starting or brokering contact with possible partners for Warnborough College. He not only calls them up on the phone or emails them he has visited quite a few in person. Whether they were Thai military generals, Catholic nuns or ruthless businessmen, Ray met them all. He was present with many key Warnborough officers at the St Paul University Philippines (a Warnborough academic partner) Centenary celebrations in 2006.

In 2007, Ray nominated Councillor Wilson for a Honoris Causa. It did not take long before this was approved by the Warnborough Council. He accompanied Councillor Wilson and his wife to Canterbury, where the convocation ceremony took place inside the beautiful and centuries-old Chapter House at Canterbury Cathedral. Ray introduced Councillor Wilson and his achievements to the audience before the Honoris Causa was bequeathed, by Trixie, Baroness Gardner – a Peer in the House of Lords, and formerly from Parkes, herself.

In the summer of 2013, Ray made his final trip to Canterbury. This time, he was to introduce Aboriginal Elder Councillor

Robert Francis Isaacs – his former prodigy – as the Honoris Causa recipient for the year. Just as they shared the same middle name, Robert too had spent the last 50 years breaking down cultural barriers and improving the lives of thousands of Aboriginal people. Thanks to Ray, he been able to go on an American exchange programme involving special projects with the Uti Indians in Utah. After his return from Utah, Robert had focused on understanding how Australian legislation and policies impacted Aboriginal people, and then developed practical, innovative policies and programs to assist them. His initiatives include establishing dental, rehabilitation and health care clinics; improving relations between Aboriginals and the justice system; assisting in establishing Clontarf Aboriginal College; and leading housing initiatives. He founded the Aboriginal Medical Service Dental Clinic. He was the first Aboriginal person to be elected to local government in his previous roles as Councillor and Deputy Mayor for the City of Gosnells. Robert pioneered the first negotiation between a multinational mining company and an Aboriginal community. He is now Executive Member to the Western Australia State Aboriginal Advisory Council (Aboriginal Affairs Planning Authority Act).

Ray bristles with pride when he recalls the proud moment he stood side-by-side with his former student. That same year (2013), Warnborough announced a scholarship in Ray's name aimed at helping talented but disadvantaged students.

In Warnborough, he had not only found a new outlet for his talents and energies – he found a new global family who shared in his vision.

With his longstanding interest in Warnborough and its alumni, Ray continues to enjoy being part of a forward-thinking institution, remaining an inspirational bedrock for the College even now, nearly twenty years later.

Chapter Five
The Whole Story
The philosophy connection
Throughout his working life, Dr Raymond Francis Morland had been one of the early motivators for education (both in New Zealand and in Western Australia). He continues in this vein to this very day.

Although Ray has held various positions during his career, the one that stands out for him is the position he held as Lecturer in Social Work at the Western Australia Institute of Technology (WAIT) in Perth. Including the promotion to Senior Lecturer for the last seven years of this position, he stayed at WAIT for a total of 11 years bringing much change to the local indigenous communities.

Ray had begun his journey into education with no real direction as to what he ultimately wanted. All he had was a clear conviction that he would, one day, 'make it!'

From boilermaker's apprentice to completing his PhD, and a two-year spell in the military, Ray looks back with a sense of bemusement.

"Not bad for a 14 year old school dropout!" he says.

In terms of philosophy, Ray has had a long-term affinity with the thoughts of St Thomas Aquinas (1225-1274). Considered one of the great medieval thinkers, Aquinas likened 'the mind at birth to a "tabula rasa" (or "blank slate"), believing that all our knowledge comes to us from our sense-experience (Philosophy, Law, S, 2007).

St Thomas, who was canonised in 1323, is also often associated with his famous quote: 'Give me the child for the first seven years, and I will show you the man.'

This is a quote frequently used by Ray. When he is asked about the person who had most influenced him throughout his life, he would mention his father first.

"I believe that I was very close to both my parents for the first thirteen years of my life. The strong influences of my childhood memories, such as my father wading through the flood waters helping people; or felling the trees in our school playground; my parents working together with a common purpose; the meetings we all attended… these are the things that have made me who I am today."

Ray has continued to do what he learned from his father's knee, all his life – helping people in need. In his case, he had used education as the tool to enhance both himself and his students for life.

There are four other people who he believes have been influential on his life. The first, being his local hairdresser Tom Brosnan, who taught him about day-to-day living. A former champion cyclist, Tom explained to Ray and his friends about the importance of eating properly, which energy-giving foods to eat, and how to stay clean and healthy. Tom also demonstrated the importance of exercising correctly and appropriately, how to understand, and use, social skills and the need for having a purpose in life. In addition, it was important to have a good attitude, be thoughtful of others, wear washed and pressed clothes and clean shoes, and be well-groomed at all times.

The adult Ray has used these pointers throughout his life; passing the skills on to others when he could, whether they were in prison or university.

The second person was Philip Ashton Smithells, "whose educational and career support for me, over many years, was quite something," says Ray. "Not only giving me advice and being there as someone for me to talk to when difficulties arose, PAS really gave me a chance. I believe I was, in some way, a fascination to PAS. I do not think that in his privileged, upper-class English background, he had come across such a rough diamond who wanted to improve his lot. PAS helped me in many ways, and even after I had graduated, he was always ready to support me. PAS called all qualified tradesmen 'artisans'. He said that because I had been such a success in the educational system, he had since been able to take on more artisans for each course."

The third person who believed in Ray was Jim Caughly. Jim had been the Chief Psychologist in the Department of Justice, where, with the help of Smithells, Ray got his first job following graduation. "Jim was one of the men who, during the war, had made major decisions within the military, such as determining who would be 'dropped' behind enemy lines in Europe. He saw my potential, and in many ways, helped my many bosses to see my potential too," says Ray.

The fourth person of note to Ray was Eric Atkinson, the Head of the Department of Psychology and Social Work at WAIT. He not only kept the peace within the university, in spite of the politics, but he encouraged Ray and helped to bring Ray's ideas of the Aboriginal courses and seminars to fruition. He had been a Lieutenant Colonel in the Western Command of the Australian Army.

Ray, in other people's words

As much as Ray has been influenced by the people in his life, others have looked to Ray for inspiration and as a role model. The following testimonies underline that significance.

For David and Betsy Buchanan, long-standing friends of the Morland family, Ray stands as an inspiration, not only to themselves, but also to the students he has taught throughout the years.

David worked on the various welfare programmes with Ray in WAIT. He says: *"The indigenous statistics in Western Australia today, still leave room for improvement, but, in many cases, the leadership of the indigenous community came through the bridging courses. The Welfare Practice Programme, which I co-ordinated, in close co-operation with Ray, was a development of the bridging course."*

"Without Ray's advocacy, and regardless of the amount of support the Academic Staff Association gave to his work, the indigenous programmes were moved to the University of Western Australia, although some of the Social Work graduates did come through the Social Work programme at WAIT."

"The decision to close the enclave in South Australia was based on the changes in the educational system that made a one entry point support enclave outdated. I believe Ray will be seen as a very significant figure due to his remarkable rapport with the indigenous community in Western Australia, which has seen terrible social statistics. It was an amazing achievement to get the indigenous community behind the bridging courses, and to mobilise them around issues to do with Landrights and Mining, which are the big issues in Western Australia."

According to David, Ray did a lot of the work in his own time, with very little support, and with much opposition, from the bulk of the relevant professions. Following his departure from WAIT, the University set up an indigenous studies centre, also establishing the bridging courses, now staffed by the same people Ray had trained a few years before.

"I felt Ray's industrial experience, his work as a physical educator, his sporting accomplishments, and cultural background, all contributed to his achievements. Above all, Ray had an indefinable quality of remaining focused despite setbacks; in this, he showed extraordinary self-discipline," says David.

At the time, it was very hard to assist indigenous Western Australians. Yet, the indigenous community had always acknowledged Ray's unique contribution to their education and welfare. He not only helped with education, but also by pushing the boundaries into public health systems and welfare state issues for the indigenous people.

To assist with this research, Betsy and David kindly provided a copy of a letter sent in 2015 by an indigenous patient to his surgeon in Western Australia. The patient, who had received the first double transplant in the 1990s, sent the letter to update his surgeon on his progress.

The patient wrote thanking the surgeon for the '*double transplant – liver and kidneys, performed in 1998.*' He also mentioned that he '*was doing a lot of work in the community, such as, voluntary work, working with the Red Cross, and with the local Aboriginal Centre.*'

The letter then mentions Betsy Buchanan, and how, through her wonderful work, over decades, she helped Noongar families in Western Australia before closing with:

'I decided to take this opportunity to get in touch with you through her (Betsy), to say thank you for what you did for me.'

In a roundabout way, the letter confirms how Ray's work continues, even to this day. However, without his understanding of the indigenous cultures, and the determination to make changes, such medical interventions would possibly not have happened.

David believes that "*we could never have done the work we did without his help and support. He gave of himself selflessly over our lifetime, and was more than a mentor. A physician who saw the (above) letter commented that without a public system and some kind of welfare state, very few indigenous clients would get transplants in the vascular surgery area. I worked as a social worker on the vascular surgery unit in the Royal Perth Hospital, and the Consultants made themselves available to the 'poorest of the poor' after surgery, as rehabilitation was so difficult to come by."*

Betsy Buchanan received a Honoris Causa Doctorate from Warnborough in 2006, in honour of her work with the Aboriginal Community, which has spanned over 40 years. This was due to Ray's proposal to the Warnborough College Council.

On 8 March 2017, Dr Betsy Buchanan was inducted into the Western Australia Women's Hall of Fame. She was honoured for her work in legal and human rights fields, particularly her tireless advocacy work with the Noongar Aboriginal community.

In an interview with Warnborough College, Betsy mentions her gratitude to Ray for getting her the honorary degree. "It has certainly helped with the people I work with a lot, especially when I had to deal with the housing authorities and they were very keen to evict people," she chuckles wryly.

There were schools of social work or orientations in social work in Australia. While Ray was in harmony with these ideals, the general approach in social work education was 'pretty indifferent' to social policy.

Traditional social work offered very little to indigenous clients as their own culture was so inaccessible to dynamic counselling techniques. While the policies were later accepted, Ray had faced enormous opposition for much of his career.

Kevin Wringe remembers Ray from his time at WAIT. In an email sent to the author in September 2015, Kevin said:

"I first met Raymond Morland in 1971, when I applied to the Western Australian Institute of Technology (WAIT) for admission

into the four years full-time Bachelor Degree course in Social Work. Ray was on the admissions panel, which conducted the initial interviews, as part of the assessment process for admission to this course. During the years 1972 – 1976 inclusive, I completed the Bachelor of Social Work degree and the Bachelor of Arts (Social Science) degree at WAIT, which later was renamed Curtin University, located in Bentley, WA. During this extensive period of time, Ray Morland was Senior Lecturer in Social Work, through which I attended many lectures given by him and I engaged in many conversations with him.

Following graduation, I had contact with Ray at various times, including conducting a joint radio interview with him on the important subject of unemployed persons, whilst I was employed with the Department of Employment and Youth Affairs. Subsequently, during my time as a social worker in Bunbury in WA's South West Region, I had further contact with Ray, although irregular contact at that point in time. Later on, I met Ray in Perth during several visits by him to WA, when we engaged in conversations regarding the community services sector. I have kept up contact with Ray over many years, including through email in recent years.

I valued Ray Morland's qualities of deep integrity, his strong commitment to the marginalized in society, his compassion for underprivileged people, his sound values, and his groundedness. I have always found Ray to be approachable, a very good listener and communicator, and one whose values I deeply respected. He was always passionate in his strong commitment to his profession, to the community services sector, and the marginalised in society.

Based on my professional studies at WAIT (Curtin University), which I consider to be very significant and very important, along with my own dedication and commitment, I was able to work in the community services sector with significant skills, through which I made an impact across the sector, including in case work, group work, community work and in welfare administration. As a graduate I worked in the Commonwealth Public Sector, the State Public Sector, the non government sector, and later on as a director in Wringe & Wringe Consulting. I worked with indigenous communities, as well as in rural areas and across the metropolitan area of Perth. I headed up various districts and specialist branches in the State community services department, as well as a large non government sector umbrella body. I was a 1988 Churchill Fellow which enabled me to undertake a study tour of crisis intervention services in the USA, UK and Ireland. I emphasise the point here that all of this was based on my initial professional training and learning which I acquired at WAIT, including significantly through Ray Morland, Senior Lecturer in Social Work there.

I have been most interested with and impressed by Ray Morland's commitment in the community services sector, and especially his support for the marginalised and social justice issues, including in his senior years. He once wrote to me in recent years of his 'refirement' instead of 'retirement,' a concept which I liked, was impressed with and have been inspired by as I now undertake voluntary work in my retirement, with Jesuit Social Services in the role of Perth Coordinator of Jesuit Volunteers Australia, and in my other commitments.

I sincerely congratulate Ray Morland for his long, sustained and passionate commitment to the community services sector, especially through tertiary education but also through social action and in various other ways, over a long period of time. I am deeply grateful to him for the part he played in my professional development and formation, and for his ongoing encouragement and inspiration, including in recent years when others of his age would have long ago fully retired. I wish him well following a long life in which he has contributed to many over a very extensive period of time."

Councillor Jill Hall from the Australian Labor Party in Newcastle wrote on 14 November 2016:

"I first met Raymond Morland when I became the Federal Member for Shortland in 1998, although I previously had contact with him when he worked at the Newcastle University, and right from that first meeting he was an inspiration.

I was at an AL Branch meeting and this elderly Branch Member with a New Zealand accent proceeded to question my report, Federal Labor's policies and the New South Wales Branch of the Labor Party. Not only did he question, he also put forward solutions. Of course, this was Ray Morland - a person I regard as a friend and a role model.

He is someone I really respect. He is a thinker, an innovator, he has true Labor values and he has spent his whole life fighting to make the world and Australia, a better place whilst at the same time pushing for reform within his Australian Labor Party, a Party of which he is a Life Member.

It is inspirational to meet and work with someone like Ray. He fights for change creatively and he determinedly maintains his strong values. If only there were more Ray Morlands, the world would be more dynamic. He challenged the odds a Catholic boy in a largely Protestant town from a working-class background who has a lifetime of achievement yet is still committed to his original values."

Dr Alexander Beveridge is the Emeritus Academic on the Discipline of Community Welfare and Human Services at the University of Newcastle. In his personal reflections, this is what he has to say about Ray.

Throughout my years as a student drawing on Dr Morland's expertise and practical wisdom, what struck me most significantly was his strengths-based approach, which seized not on our deficits but rather encouraged our potential and capacity to increase our effort. This was effected largely by Dr Morland's ability to stimulate student interest and to see the connections between otherwise bland content knowledge and the world of social welfare practice.

Regardless of whether our future practice interests were working with individuals in counselling, or families, or in social administration roles, the emphasis Dr Morland placed was always on integrating wide knowledge and taking a critical approach. Consistently throughout my years of study and mentoring, Dr Morland challenged taken-for-granted ways of thinking – the key maxim espoused by Dr Morland was: 'rather than rushing to diagnose/assess personal pathologies/troubles it is important to look beyond so as to grasp the underlying structural issues of poverty, social dislocation/exclusion, ageism, gender, race, geographical isolation, and so on. For many graduates, this was to provide an empowering and more reflexive approach to supporting clients impacted by myriad social problems.

Personally, I, and so many graduates who have taken their place in senior social administration, juvenile justice, health, migrant services, domestic violence support services, refuges for the homeless and many more practice contexts, owe Dr Morland a great debt not only for the expertise and critical thinking skills imparted but also the passionate philosophical values and tenets centred on anti-oppressive practice, and the need for a personal commitment to affecting social-change.

At no time during Dr Morland's tenure as Head of Department, community activist and lobbyist, nor classroom-teacher did he embrace a passive approach. Indeed, collectively as graduates we remember with pride the effort, the humour, the empathy for the socially excluded at centre of Dr Morland's positivistic approach and philosophy. Clearly, such ideas undoubtedly parallel Abraham Maslow, in particular, the inherent worth of each and every individual, and so too, the belief that all people if given the right chances and social/emotional support will have the capacity to achieve their highest goals.

From the perspective of my own academic career of 33 years, influenced and supported greatly by Dr Morland, I continue to draw of the central tenets and empowering approaches founded in those years as a student. Dr Morland, while confronting comfort-zones of everyday thinking, challenged us to see beyond the rigid formulaic approaches underpinning so many social services. Rather than taking a punitive, largely controlling function with our clients, we were inspired to believe in, and to seek-out potential social change.

I would strongly suggest that Dr Morland's contribution and life-long inspiration has been at the centre of much substantive efforts by graduates often working with clients in dire social situations. In sum, the life and times of Dr Morland did not end with formal retirement from academic life. His inspiration and positivistic approach has rippled-out throughout the social welfare community and improved the lives of countless individuals, families, and communities. Without question, an academic and social activist can achieve no greater outcome.

Professor William Cook has been friends with Ray for a very long time. They worked together at the University of Newcastle, and here is what he has to say about Ray:

Professor Raymond Morland has been a dedicated, intuitive and active university academic. During his involvement at a high level of tertiary education, he has developed and supervised the implementation of course structures in both Perth & Newcastle universities. Social welfare has been his principal area of expertise. Similarly, his involvement with Warnborough College has involved the role of Council Secretary, international graduation ceremonies, and guidance in organisational development. He utilises a high level of interpersonal help with students and individuals in need. To support this, Ray has been involved in community work with organisations like the Salvation Army. He has always encouraged post-graduate studies and has been both mentor and examiner. I congratulate Professor Ray Morland in relation to his numerous achievements.

Dr John Allen, the Chairman of the Warnborough College Council has this to say about Ray:

I first met Ray in 2001. He impressed me with his enthusiasm for Warnborough, particularly its global vision. He said he wanted to be part of 'the team' given his wide background in international education, and his experience in helping Australian aborigines aspire to further education. In 2003, Ray was elected to the Warnborough Council. Since then, Ray has attended Council meetings and graduations around the world. I have appreciated and valued his wisdom and support throughout the last 16 years. Ray is a remarkable educator and one whose membership the Council has had the privilege of working with.

Canon Rev'd Dr Richard G. Martin, Warnborough College Chaplain, wraps up succinctly about Ray:

Although Ray was never fond of shellfish, the world became his oyster. His global connections have been useful at every level - professional, academic and political. Learning across borders has been a special focus, and his wide network has enabled students to benefit from his many contacts and wisdom.

In recent decades Warnborough College with its philosophy of global learning provided a special point of focus for the education-related causes most dear to Raymond's vision and, doubtless, the President and the Board Members of the College, its faculty, alumni, students and friends will derive much benefit, indeed pearls of wisdom, from their reading of this book.

These testimonials show just how much of an inspiration Dr Ray Morland has been to others, who themselves, have gone on to inspire and impact on their own contacts. It goes to show that just as there were people who opened the door for Ray, he too has opened the door for many.

Ray, in his own words

"I make no apologies for being a Socialist, not as my father was over eighty years ago, but one who is living in the 21st Century, well aware that times have changed. I am also not a dreamer, because the reality of life gives us no time to dream. To quote Thomas Jefferson (1743 – 1826), possibly amongst others: 'There is nothing more unequal than the equal treatment of unequal people.' I know this attitude has come from my early experiences, as a child, growing up in a working class family; my time in the boiler shops, being involved with the trade unions; on the ships during the war; seeing for myself the poor working conditions and the destruction in Korea and other countries, with wars still going on.

The poverty I witnessed, when in the Philippines, Thailand, and Indonesia, is poverty that should not still be happening, but is. Such countries themselves are often rich, but the riches do not appear to be reaching the people in true need. Our governments can spend billions of dollars finding water on Mars, but we cannot find water in parts of Africa, which could save thousands of lives!

My story is not unique, but as I look back over my life, I recognise the lasting imprint of my parents. I thank them for the example of the lives they lived, right out in front of us children, and the encouragement they gave us, by word and example, to value the things that mattered to them. I hope my life has reflected some of those values."

Author's Notes: Full Circle

Looking back on the life of Dr Raymond Francis Morland has been a privilege. The educational threads run through everything he has done, even though he never wanted to be in the educational field initially.

The testaments above clearly show Ray's inspirational and motivational impact on his fellow human beings. Indeed, he has broken down barriers between different cultures, established solid educational programmes for indigenous communities, and dared to stand up to indifference amongst his own peers.

Perhaps Ray's sensibilities for education, experience and adventure comes from his forebears, namely his grandfather, who moved to New Zealand from Northern Ireland in search of a better life. Likewise, his father, on a whaling ship in search of something different. Ray simply does not believe in giving up. When the going gets tough, he just carries on.

It goes without saying then, that the people he most appreciated and admired in life were the ones who 'did not give up.' It did not matter who - friends, work colleagues, students, or family. This list includes his wife, Lynn, the woman who has stood shoulder-to-shoulder with him for the last fifty-five years.

Like his father before him, Ray has been involved with the Australian Labor Party and trade unions for over 70 years (35 of these in Newcastle, Australia).

Ray developed his administrative and leadership expertise to bolster social welfare agencies in the fields of motivation, personal growth and development. He is widely-published on social issues, and frequently been invited to read papers at international conferences. The World Health Organisation has recognised Ray's research into alcohol abuse reduction strategies as a most significant contribution to Aboriginal welfare.

Ethyl M. Tempest-Mogg was the pioneer in international education who founded Warnborough College on a dream of making it possible to educate students worldwide. This ethos was to be achieved by 'crossing boundaries and widening horizons' and this motto resonated with Ray's own experience – daring to cross his own, working class tracks in his thirst for knowledge, while enabling others to do the same.

As Secretary to the Warnborough College Council, Ray has been a dependable stalwart. Nowadays, with over ninety years under his belt, Ray is the voice of wisdom for many of the Warnborough alumni. Never one to keep still, he enjoys following the Rugby Union, listening to classical music, and keeping abreast of current affairs.

"He who opens a school door closes a prison." Victor Hugo

About the Author

Pamela Hatton has spent all her working life in healthcare. Apart from her general practice work covering all aspects of individual behaviours and functioning, her main areas of focus have been on self-image, domestic violence, and inappropriate behaviours in the workplace. To date, her written work has focused mainly on nursing standards, and mobbing and bullying in the workplace.

Disclaimer

The majority of the research undertaken for this work has been through email, with Dr Morland, his friends and colleagues, and internet searches. Although researching the facts, for dates, educational establishments, qualification dates, and levels, was attempted, the author would be most appreciative of any further information referring to the persons named, and to the content of this work. Should a reader find factual, and or other discrepancies within this work, the author would be most obliged if the person or persons informed the publisher directly, thereby allowing for the discrepancy to be righted. There has been no intention to mislead, or to give, or to use, incorrect information.
Dr Pamela Hatton

www.ingramcontent.com/pod-product-compliance
Ingram Content Group UK Ltd.
Pitfield, Milton Keynes, MK11 3LW, UK
UKHW020237250726
13967UKWH00001B/410

9 780956 866752